TRAVIS & FREDDY'S
Adventures in Vegas

Pi Pie & a Raptor

Walla Walla Junior High School trembles in terror. And no one's trembling more than Travis Best. Travis is an easy-on-the-eyes guy with naturally perfect hair and a million-dollar smile. He's one of those people who can talk his way into, or out of, anything. During his short yet eventful life, Travis has already: 1) thrown a no-hitter; 2) scored a game-winning goal on a diving header; 3) nailed a three-pointer as the clock was running out. So why does a gnarly, butt-clenching dread gnaw at his guts? Because Travis Best is staring down his natural enemy.

A killer math test.

And he is utterly unprepared. In fairness, even with maximum preparation, numbers slide like ice off the glassy surface of his brain. Many times in his brief but spectacularly bad academic career, Travis has tried studying. Unfortunately, no matter how hard he studies, numbers continue to swim in his head, wiggling and wriggling so he can't ever quite catch them.

But today he has hope. This hope can be found on his

face, where a pair of extra-large, super-sparkly, crazy-pointy, cat-eyed old-lady glasses are now hanging out. They're strange glasses for a twelve-year-old boy at any time, but especially when he's staring down a killer math test.

Travis Best, sitting in the second row of the classroom, turns around now and makes a funny scrunchy old-lady face, which remarkably resembles the face of their teacher, Mrs. Rappaport, the dreaded Raptor.

Eighty-four percent of the kids laugh out loud at Travis's Raptor impersonation. Not normal behavior before a killer math test. But laughter is the other side of terror.

Three and a half blocks away from Walla Walla Junior High School, at 393 Maple Street, sits a kid who was born at the exact same time and place as Travis Best.

This kid is wearing big headphones that make him look like a four-foot seven-inch member of a giant-eared race of mutant four-eyed geeks, staring at his oversize supercharged computer screen that looks like it could hack into the White House.

Frederick Xavier Quigley is the kid. Freddy to his friend. Who is Travis. Every day is a bad hair day for Freddy. It looks like weeds are sprouting out of his head, and no one has mowed the lawn in a long time. Then there's the face. Travis has the kind of face cameras love taking pictures of. Freddy, on the other hand, has one of those faces that's a natural enemy of the camera. It's a long horse face with a nose that's crazy crooked and bumpy from getting busted after he tumbled butt over handlebars in an ugly biking accident. And then there's the teeth. Big, bucked, currently covered with braces that are slowly and painfully unbucking those massive choppers, surrounding them like silver metal bumpers. A mole just above his lip looks like a small smudge of fudge waiting to be wiped off. Naturally, Freddy Quigley wears glasses with lenses so thick it looks like a couple of whale eyes are floating around in the middle of his face. Freddy can't pitch a fiery fastball, or throw a perfect spiral, or nail a three-pointer no matter how much time's left on the clock. But Freddy has a big brain. While Travis never met a number he liked, Freddy's mind eats numbers like a hungry kid alone in a bakery. Travis Best got the million-dollar smile. Freddy Quigley got the million-dollar brain. Evidence of this hangs on the wall directly behind Freddy's head, where a plaque says:

GENIUS

PRESENTED BY

MASSACHUSETTS INSTITUTE OF TECHNOLOGY

Right now Freddy's big brain is staring through his thick glasses at a slightly out-of-focus Carolyn Strummeister, who's smiling from his TV screen.

That's because Travis is staring at Carolyn Strummeister back at Walla Walla Junior High, where Travis and Carolyn are sitting, about to take their killer math test, three and a half blocks away.

That's because Freddy Quigley has used that huge brain of his to plant a microscopic fiber-optic digital-signal processor, mini-microphonic transducer, and a refractive receiver into the stems and joints of those goofy, cat-eyed, old-lady glasses. And they're connected to his turbocharged, beefed-up gigabyte liquid-cooled monster supercomputer, cyber-rigging those glasses so Freddy can see everything Travis sees, listen to everything Travis hears, and actually talk into Travis's ear, all at the same time.

This explains the hope Travis Best is feeling as he stares down the killer math test through those goofy glasses.

There's only one problem. Neither one of them is actually sure if the whole thing is going to work. And if it doesn't, there's a 99.99% chance Travis Best will fail this test, flunk math, and be sentenced to summer school, which would be a giant slice of misery.

Travis is staring at Carolyn Strummeister because he thinks she likes him. Carolyn smiles at Travis. She, too, has a million-dollar smile. In fact, she does like Travis, but she worries sometimes that he's not quite smart enough.

Travis Best himself hardly ever worries, but when he

does, that's what he worries about, too: that he's not quite smart enough.

Meanwhile, three and a half blocks away, Freddy Quigley is staring like a love puppy at Carolyn Strummeister on his giant monitor. Freddy focuses the picture so he can get a better look at the girl he's got a stupid crush on, even though she barely knows he exists.

"Ohhhhhhh, man," Freddy moans into the microphone, "so that's what it's like to have Carolyn Strummeister smile at you."

Miraculously, these words are transmitted through the old-lady glasses and straight into Travis's ear, which transports the words straight into his brain.

Travis nods his head, which makes Carolyn bob up and down on Freddy's screen.

"Hey, can you hear me?" Freddy says, all excited. "Nod your head again to confirm audio hookup."

Travis nods again, which makes Carolyn bob some more in front of Freddy, who raises his arms into the air and punches his fist there.

"Oh yeah! The Gigabyte Kid strikes again!"

Freddy stares at Carolyn Strummeister smiling at him from his computer screen.

"Think she'd ever go out with me?" he asks with moony goffiness.

"No way," Travis says out loud, shaking his head, which makes Carolyn go back and forth on Freddy's TV.

Travis realizes the entire class is looking at him.

"Don't talk to me, dimwit!" Freddy barks at him.

Travis realizes his error, smiles that big smile, and says:

"No way . . . am I failing this test."

"Smooth move, ya protozoa," Freddy sneers into Trav's ear.

Suddenly everything gets extra quiet, like in the movies right before something really bad happens. Travis feels a dark and large looming presence behind him. His spine tingles and quivers. Instinctively he turns. And yes, there she is:

Mrs. Rappaport, the dreaded Raptor, his teacher, hovering over him, ready to tear him to shreds with her razorlike claws and blade-sharp teeth.

When her sour, pinched puss appears right in Travis's face, his heart skips two beats and he stops breathing, while his guts tumble upside down.

When the dreaded Raptor, amplified to larger-than-life viciousness, fills Freddy's big screen, he bolts back in his chair, the daylights scared right out and him, as he yelps:

"YIKES!"

The dreaded Raptor stares hard, up close and personal, at Travis's old-lady glasses, practically sniffing them, trying to figure out what no-good Travis is up to.

"Travis Best," the Raptor snaps, "why are wearing those glasses?"

"Don't panic," Freddy whispers into Travis's ear. "Remain calm."

"Wellllll," Travis says to the snarling Raptor as he smiles his million-dollar smile, "my little brother sat on my regular glasses, and these are my mom's, and we have the same subscription—"

"Subscription?" the Raptor growls with a man-eating scowl.

"Prescription, ya pustule!" says Freddy.

"Prescription, ya pust—" Travis stops just before he finishes saying *pustule*.

"Yeeessss?" says the Raptor, like she'd really enjoy ripping Travis's throat out right about now.

"Puh-scription, yeah, we got the same puh-scription," says Travis smoothly.

"An excellent save by Wonder Boy Travis Best as the crowd goes crazy!" Freddy punches a button on his computer that makes the sound of a crowd going crazy, while Travis tries hard to keep from smiling.

The dreaded Raptor snarls, grabs the glasses off Travis's head, and studies them hungrily, like she wants to eat them. She's searching for a tiny little piece of paper with answers to the killer math test written in small letters on it.

Meanwhile, back on Maple Street, Freddy's getting dizzy from the picture on his screen moving around like a bad music video, in and out of focus, the class flying wildly across his big screen as the dreaded Raptor tries to catch Travis at whatever bad thing she knows he's up to.

Which of course she doesn't, because she'd never guess in a kazillion years that the goofy glasses have Travis jacked right into Freddy's big brain.

Finally, the dreaded Raptor hands the glasses back to Travis, disappointed at not catching him in the act of whatever it is he's up to. And she's certain he's up to something.

Travis puts them back on as he says:

"Why, thank you, Mrs. Rappaport. Without my glasses, I can't tell cake from pi."

Then he smiles real big as he turns to the class, and a giggle ripples through the room.

"Excellent," says Freddy, who wishes he could make people laugh *with* him instead of *at* him.

For the first time in his life, Travis looks down at a killer math test and smiles like he doesn't have a care in the world, secure in the fact that Freddy's big brain will do all the thinking for him. Again.

Meanwhile, back at Command Central, the math test looks fuzzy on Freddy's big screen, but that's only because the autofocus in the magical glasses hasn't kicked in yet.

Once it does, Freddy's big brain immediately de-gobbledygooks it.

There isn't a killer math test Freddy can't kill.

"Okay, here we go," says Freddy. "Number one: 3 Y squared."

Travis writes: 3 Y □

"You don't write down a square for squared, you write down a small two next to the Y, dog breath," Freddy says.

"Hey, stick—" Travis starts to say something rude to Freddy, but Quigley quickly cuts him off.

"No talking!" Freddy really enjoys the fact that for once in his life he gets the last word with Travis.

Travis erases the square box and writes: $3Y^2$.

"All right." Freddy's back to all-business. "Number two: 1 X over Y.

"Number three: negative 1.

"Number four: pi equals 3.14159265358979323846 2643383279502884197169399375."

When Travis gets to number four, he draws a little apple pie, fresh from the oven, with stream rising off it. It looks like this:

"You don't draw a pie, ya warthog," Freddy sneers. "Draw two straight lines coming down, with a squiggly line over it. Must be tough having moldy cheese where a brain should be."

Normally, Travis would now make a wisecrack that would make Freddy the butt of a joke. If you've ever been used as a butt, you know what a pain it can be.

But this time, Travis Best bites his tongue, swallows, and erases his little drawing of a slice of pie, replacing it with the symbol for pi, which looks like this:

$$\pi$$

Travis finishes the test in sixteen minutes and four seconds.

"Okay, extra credit," says Freddy.

Travis Best's eyes go wide. Usually he doesn't even get regular credit, never mind *extra* credit.

"X plus ½ times 3."

Travis writes down the extra credit extra carefully. Then he strides the test over to the Raptor and plops it on her desk with a fine flourish.

The dreaded Raptor's sour face goes all scrunchy, like she just sucked on a rotten lemon, which makes Freddy burst out laughing in his room three and a half blocks away. Naturally, Freddy has a gawky geek of a laugh. It's very loud and it sounds like this.

"HAR HAR HAR—SNORT!"

When Travis turns around and flashes that million-dollar smile, knowing he just aced the killer math test, the class looks like a school of shocked twelve-year-old largemouth bass.

A warm feeling sweeps over Travis. He usually gets this feeling on a baseball diamond, a football field, or a basketball court. This is the first time he's ever had it in a classroom. And he likes it. A lot.

Travis puts a thumb up in front of the glasses, takes them off, stares slyly into them at arm's length, and mouths to Freddy:

"Thanks, man!"

Freddy, back at Command Central, says:

"My pleasure, Trav."

Travis folds the goofy glasses and carefully pockets them.

Unfortunately, when he does this, massive feedback causes an ear-piercing screech to jolt Freddy right out of his chair and tumbles him to the floor as he tries ripping the big headphones off his ears while shouting:

"TAKE THE GLASSES OUT OF YOUR POCKET!"

Travis smiles at Carolyn Strummeister, unable to hear Freddy's muffled voice yelling at him from inside his pocket.

Freddy doesn't see it, but Carolyn Strummeister smiles back.

A Goober, a Lock & a Hydra

On the playground outside Walla Walla Junior High School, Travis is tossing a football with his jockster buddies Big Brad, who's big, and Fast Phil, who's fast.

"Travis Best, why are you wearing those glasses?" Trav does a spot-on impersonation of their teacher.

"Dude, you sound exactly like the dreaded Raptor," chuckles Fast Phil.

"Exactly," laughs Big Brad.

"I aced that test," brags Travis.

"Yeah, right," snorts Fast Phil, not buying a word of it.

"I'm getting an A," says Trav. "It's a lock."

"No way the King of the Idiots is gettin' an A," says Big Brad.

"Not happ'nin'," says Fast Phil.

"Put yer money where yer mouth is." Travis smiles like a guy who's about to win a bet. "Ten bucks says I get an A."

"Ten bucks? Sign me up," says Big Brad.

"This is gonna be the easiest ten bucks I ever made," says Fast Phil.

They follow this with a jumping high-five.

This is a lock, thinks Travis. A solid lock. If there's one thing Travis has learned from his dad, it's that there's nothing as sweet as a solid lock.

A small gangly goober appears in the distance.

"Hey, look, it's Dr. Doofus!" Fast Phil points.

"Hey, Dr. Doofus! Catch!" shouts Big Brad.

Big Brad chucks the football hard and true at the head of Freddy, who puts his dinky hands up to catch it. Naturally, the ball flies straight through his hands and smack-dabs him right between the eyes.

This noise comes out of Freddy:

"Owwoofouchyeowohhhhhhhhh!"

He crumbles, clutching the thick forehead that, luckily for him, protects his big brain.

Travis scowls at Big Brad and Fast Phil, who laugh in that special way big stupid guys do when they humiliate little smart guys.

"You're such a Hydra," he spits with disgust at Big Brad.

"A what?" Big Brad asks.

"A Hydra," Travis says.

"What's that?" Big Brad asks.

"Look it up." Travis smirks as he walks away from Big Brad and Fast Phil with a disgusted shake of his head.

A Hydra is, in fact, a many-headed monster that grows back two heads for every one you chop off.

Travis only knows this because Freddy has made him learn one new word every day for the last six months.

Travis used to really hate learning all those words, but now as he walks toward Freddy, he thinks: Dude, that was cool.

"You okay?" Travis asks. As he helps his best friend up, he notices a perfect little cross in the middle of Freddy's forehead where the football crash-landed into it.

Freddy Quigley, recipient of so much jock-generated grief, is very happy that Travis Best, master athlete, is his best friend.

He feels around in his brain. Everything seems okay. So he says:

"Yeah, I'm okay."

Suddenly Carolyn Strummeister turns a corner with Caitlin Montgomery and Missy Richardson, who rank number two and three in popularity among twelve-year-old girls at WW Junior High. Right behind Carolyn, who is clearly numero uno.

When Freddy sees Carolyn, he immediately starts worrying that despite his big brain, he's going to say something stupid. That makes his glands begin working overtime, pumping out smelly sweat as his legs beg to back away.

Travis sees his friend melting down, so he steps in, like he always does.

"Carolyn, this is my best friend, Freddy." Travis smiles that million-dollar smile, causing all three girls to sigh inside.

Freddy, meanwhile, smiles his ten-cent smile, hair sticking up like a scarecrow in bad repair.

"I didn't know you guys were such good friends," says Carolyn.

Carolyn, Caitlin, and Missy study Freddy, suddenly thinking that maybe he's an adorable shy guy in need of a new haircut, and not necessarily the loser of the universe.

"Oh yeah," says Travis, "we've got the same birthday."

"Cool." All three girls nod at the same time.

"Yeah, it's uh . . . pleasure to nice you . . . I mean, good to, uh . . . I mean, happy to . . . pleasure you—" Freddy stops when he realizes he's completely mucked it up. But of course, by that time, it's way too late.

Travis does a tiny eye-roll that nobody else sees.

"So, what are you guys doing this weekend?" asks Carolyn nicely.

"Uh, yeah, uh, yeah, uh . . ." Freddy can't even make it to the first word of this sentence.

Luckily, his best friend is there to save the day.

"Why," says Trav, "what's up?"

"I'm having a party at my house on Saturday night, you guys should come," says Carolyn.

"REA-LLY?" Freddy's voice cracks like thin ice.

The girls giggle.

Travis shoots Freddy a shut-up-while-you're-still-ahead look.

Freddy shuts up and turns purply-reddishly-crimson.

"We'd love to." Travis smiles.

Freddy tries to smile like Travis, but on him it looks more like he ate too much cabbage.

"Cool." All three girls nod like beautiful bobble-head dolls.

"Cool." Travis nods easy.

When he sees that Freddy has turned into a lifelike statue of a grinning idiot, he grabs his best friend's arm.

This kick-starts Freddy's massive brain, which orders his mouth to say:

"Indubitably."

Everybody laughs, even Freddy.

As Travis drags Freddy away, they have no idea that in less than forty-eight hours, very large and very bad men will be dangling them in their underpants out the thirty-fifth floor window of a hotel in Las Vegas.

A Polyp, a Plan & 151 Pieces of Bart Simpson

travis's room looks like a sporting-goods store threw up in it: gloves and cleats, bats and balls of the soccer, tennis, basket, foot, and base variety, all mingling with pictures of players alley-ooping, heaving Hail Marys, and flashing across the finish line.

The only thing not related to the throwing, hitting, or shooting of balls is a large map of CyberWorld, which is pinned in the middle of Travis's wall.

In one week, Travis and Freddy will turn **THIRTEEN!** All they want is to spend that birthday at CyberWorld, the hottest theme park in America.

"YOUR MIND IS THE FINAL FRONTIER!"

That's CyberWorld's motto. Using the newest virtual-reality technology, you can swing through Manhattan like Spider-Man, kill villains with your retractable titanium claws like the Wolverine, or be a Jedi knight and slice up Stormtroopers with your very own light saber. Not to mention the mind-blasting high-tech rides that spin, speed, flume, and plummet fun seekers at gut-busting speeds.

"So," says Travis, "your old man definitely won't spring for CyberWorld?"

"Are you nuts?" says Freddy. "He can barely remember to put his pants on before he leaves the house. He's a node—"

"A polyp—" says Travis.

"A streptococcus—" says Freddy.

"But thirteen, man, that's huge," groans Travis, "and we're gonna end up at Chuck E. Cheese."

"There's no possibility that your parents will change their minds?" Freddy knows the answer to that question before he even asks it.

"No way, man," Travis tosses back the tired answer.

They sit in a silence only best friends can sit in.

"Hey dude, thanks for helpin' me with the math test," says Travis. "That was way cool."

"My pleasure," says Freddy.

"Do you think it's weird?" asks Travis.

"What?" answers Freddy.

"That of all the people in the world, we got born on the exact same day, at the exact same time, in the exact same hospital?" Travis spends quite a bit of time thinking about this, trying to figure out whether it's part of some grand master plan. He secretly believes he and

Freddy are destined to do something great. He just has no idea what that might be.

Freddy doesn't think about things like that. His big brain is too busy thinking, then saying, things like this:

"Factoring in how many minutes there are in a given year, and how many people are born in that given year, the chances of any two people being born in rooms right next to each other in the same hospital at the same time would obviously be infinitesimal."

"No way, man, they've gotta be, like, really really small," Travis utters with utter sincerity.

"*Infinitesimal means* small, you mung bean," shoots back Freddy.

"Doi! Psyche!" Travis is most happy when he catches Freddy being a know-it-all.

"Booooys," Mrs. Best sings up the stairs from the kitchen, "could you come down here?"

Mrs. Best, with her extremely large hair and heart, adds two glasses of cold milk to the warm chocolate-chip cookies already on the table.

"Thanks, Mom," Travis says.

"Yeah, thanks, Mrs. B," says Freddy, who has no mom except for Mrs. B. Freddy lost his mom a long time ago. You'd think it would be very hard to lose a mom.

And it is.

Travis Best and Freddy Quigley attack the cookies

furiously, sloshing down their milk chasers, making many happy sounds.

When Mrs. Best looks at Freddy, all goofy with chocolate gooped on his face, her heart aches for this ugly duckling, and she hopes she can figure out a way to make a manly swan out of him sometime soon.

Freddy's mom died soon after giving birth to him at the exact same time that Mrs. Best was giving birth to Travis. From that day on, Mrs. Best has thought of Freddy as her own.

Like Travis, she too thinks quite a bit about the peculiar events of their birth. How like twins the boys are. Or maybe two sides of the same coin. Mrs. Best also secretly believes her boys are destined to do great things together. She too has no clue what those things might be.

"Travis, I'm so proud of you. An A-plus. I still can't believe it. You've never even gotten a B in math. You're always talking about getting a sports scholarship, but you've gotta have the grades, too. And Freddy, thanks again for all your help."

Travis and Freddy look at each other, trying to keep from busting out laughing.

"My pleasure, Mrs. B," says Freddy, doing his best I'm-a-humble-boy-genius.

"I owe it all to Freddy, Mom." Travis and Freddy, full of cookies and milk, grin at each other.

"Traaa-vis!" Mr. Best bellows from his den.

This makes Travis bite his tongue, as his eyes freak while fear fills them.

Freddy hates it when he sees that look in his best friend's face. As wacky a scatterbrain as Freddy's old man is, at least he doesn't have a temper. Trav's dad, on the other hand, has a nasty bad temper.

Travis slowly shuffles down the hall, Freddy his shadow, Scared and Witless side by side. They stop just outside the den, watching Mr. Best bark into the phone:

"I want the whole bundle on Candy Man in the third. Yeah, Whitey, let it ride. I'm tellin' ya, it's a lock, a solid lock. Don't worry, I'm good for it, just make the bet."

Mr. Best grunts into the phone a couple more times and slams it into its crib.

"You boys come in, we need to have a little talk," he says in a dark voice that sends shivers creeping like spiders down their spines.

Suddenly it's clear: they've been caught, they'll be disgraced and expelled for cheating on the math test. And no telling what Mr. Best will do when he blows his stack and the top of his head pops off.

The den is a swamp of racing forms, tip sheets, and copies of *Gambler's Monthly,* while on the TV a video called *How to Win in Vegas* blares.

When Mr. Best spins around in his chair, the boys flinch backward without meaning to.

"So, Trav," he starts, "I understand you got a little help on your math test. Is this true?"

Busted!

Travis and Freddy look at each other out of their eye corners with hands-in-the-cookie-jar faces, mumbling:

"Uh, well, yeah, uh, the thing is—"

"Is this true Travis . . . Freddy?" Mr. Best demands.

"Uh, well, yeah, uh, the thing is—" they mutter.

"I want to know exactly what kind of help you gave Travis, Freddy," says Mr. Best.

"Uh, well, yeah, uh, the thing is—" Freddy muffles.

"You were barely passing math, and all of a sudden, out of nowhere, you get an A-plus? Travis, I want to know how you explain that." Mr. Best squints at the boys.

"Uh, well, yeah, uh, the thing is—" Travis murmurs.

"Well, you boys leave me no choice." Mr. Best shakes his head hard.

"We do?" quivers Travis.

"Do we?" whispers Freddy.

"I'm taking you both . . ." he says sternly.

Travis and Freddy freeze.

". . . to CyberWorld for your birthday." Mr. Best says it like he's still mad at them, so they don't realize he's switcheroo'd 'em.

The boys continue to cringe.

Mr. Best laughs big.

"I'm taking you boys to CyberWorld for your birthday, don't you understand? I'm just about to come into some . . . good fortune, and I want you boys—I'm sorry, you young *men*—to know how much I appreciate all the hard work you've been doing."

The boys slowly go from scared, to stunned, to dumb, to numb, and they do it together, without saying a word.

This makes Mr. Best laugh harder still as he says:

"Well heck, aren't you fellas excited?"

"Uh, yeah, sure, thanks," Travis and Freddy say, afraid if they make too much noise they'll wake up and their beautiful dream will morph into a nightmare.

Together they slide quietly out of the room, fly up the stairs, and careen into Travis's room.

Once there, they bump fists, then chests, snap fingers into six-shooters, then blow the smoke away, a move they've been refining for twelve years.

Travis holds a fake mike under Freddy's mouth and says:

"So, Freddy Quigley, you and Travis Best just got named co-MVPs of the Super Bowl. What are ya gonna do now?"

"We're goin' to CyberWorld," Freddy grins.

"Your mind is the final frontier!" they chant together.

Travis and Freddy do a little happy dance while visions of dodging slow-motion bullets in the Matrix, invading the Death Star, and driving a flying car dance in their heads.

And just as all seems right in the world of Travis Best and Freddy Quigley, they hear an angry sound that shivers their timbers.

"AHHHHHHHHHHHH!"

Travis and Freddy look at each other in bug-eyed horror.

Twenty-three seconds later, cold with fear, they creep down the stairs and poke their heads into Mr. Best's office.

Freddy looks at Travis and sees his best friend more scared than he's ever seen him. This, in turn, terrifies Freddy.

"But you said it was a lock," bellows Mr. Best, "a total lock, that's what you said. Well, what exactly does *lock* mean to you? Because to me, this was not a lock. The only thing that seems to be a lock around here is your brain. . . . Hello? Hello?"

Mr. Best smashes the phone down.

CRASH!

Immediately it rings.

RING.

Mr. Best reaches for the phone. Stops.

RING.

This time he snatches it up.

"Hello? Whitey, uh, no. No, no, no. 'Cuz I can't right now. Listen, ya gotta give me a couple of days. Please,

I'm beggin' ya. Don't hang up on me, Whitey. Hello? Hello? Hello?"

Mr. Best drops the phone with a groan.

Trav's dad says in a whisper voice:

"I can't believe this is happening to me."

Travis and Freddy look at each other with a deep dish of despair.

They've never seen him this shook up before.

Mrs. Best runs in from the kitchen, saying:

"George! Is everything okay? GEORGE!"

Mr. Best doesn't answer, his face glazed like a day-old doughnut.

Mrs. Best walks past Travis and Freddy like they're not there. She stops in front of Mr. Best, whose head is drowning in his hands.

"George," says Mrs. Best, "what's wrong?"

"I lost," says Mr. Best, although if you weren't listening closely, you never woulda heard him.

"What?" Mrs. Best asks again, even though she already knows what he said.

"I lost, I lost, I lost, I lost, I lost, I lost—" says Mr. Best.

"Please stop saying that, George." Mrs. Best finally cuts him off. "It'll be okay."

Mrs. Best doesn't know it yet, but she's wrong.

It won't be okay. Not this time.

"You don't understand. I. LOST. **EVERYTHING!!!**"

Mr. Best shouts past the top of his lungs. Then his face falls into his hands, and he shakes with sobs.

Travis has never seen his dad cry. He doesn't know what to do. But he knows he can't stand there looking at his mom's face, all twisted tight, tears pooling in the blue of her eyes.

And Freddy can't stand looking at Trav's face. Seeing tears clouding there makes tears appear in Freddy's eyes.

Suddenly Mr. Best realizes Travis and Freddy are watching him break down.

"Trav, I'm really . . . sorry. Freddy, I . . ." He can't finish.

"It'll be okay, Dad." Travis says this because his mom said it.

He doesn't know it yet either, but he's wrong, too.

It so won't be okay.

"Trav," says Mr. Best, "I'm so . . ."

The misery on his sad son's face makes the words dry up between his heart and his mouth.

"I've gotta . . . get out of here." Mr. Best gets up and starts to walk out.

Mrs. B tries to stop him, but he walks past her, dazed and confused, toward the front door.

"Wait . . . George, I'm coming with you," Mrs. Best says. She's worried her husband will do something crazy if he gets behind the wheel of their car in a state of agitation.

She's right to worry.

She kisses Travis on the head and says:

"Travis honey, I want you to stay with Freddy for the weekend, okay?"

She kisses Freddy on the head.

She looks at them with as much everything's-gonna-be-all-right as she can muster. It's not nearly as much as she'd hoped. Then she says:

"Okay?"

"Okay," say Travis and Freddy at exactly the same time.

Mrs. Best gives them both a squeeze of love. Then she grabs her husband's jacket and her purse and busts out the door after him.

Unseen by Mrs. Best, her husband's wallet glides gracefully out of his jacket pocket and lands lightly on the floor beside the back door, flopping open so a gold credit card shimmy-shines in a shaft of sunlight showering through the window.

As soon as Mr. and Mrs. Best are gone, the house gets spooky quiet, like right before the Raptor tried to nail Travis in class.

Travis is in frozen shock. He's sure it's all his fault, but he has no idea why.

Freddy wants to help his best friend, but he has no clue what to do.

So he looks away.

And when he does, his eyes rest on the TV in Mr. Best's den.

Freddy's big brain, desperate for distraction from the pain strangling the air, is instantly intrigued when it sees:

How to Win in Vegas!

Huge piles of money appear on the TV as an extra-loud voice brays:

"Yes, you too can win BIG BIG money in Las Vegas!"

The screen splits into four parts: blackjack, craps, roulette, and a one-armed bandit.

"Trav, come here for a second," says Freddy.

"What?" says Travis, half-annoyed and half-happy to feel anything besides the rot he's sinking in.

"Look at this." Freddy points his terrible haircut at the TV, where a flashy man is explaining that anyone can win big, big money in Las Vegas.

"Yeah? And?" Travis asks, peeve seeping out of him.

"That's the solution, there it is, right in front of us, it's plain as the face on my, uh . . . whatever . . ." says Freddy.

He often finds that his mouth can't keep up with his brain.

"Freddy, what are you talking about, man?" Trav tries to drag the thought kicking and screaming out of Freddy.

"I have a plan—" Freddy starts, but Travis cuts him right off.

"Not now, Freddy—" says Travis.

"But this is the greatest plan I've ever had—" Freddy says.

"I don't want to hear it—" says Travis.

"No, this is the greatest of all plans—" Freddy says.

"I hate this plan—" says Travis.

"How can you hate this plan? You haven't even heard it yet!" asks Freddy.

"Trust me, I hate it," says Travis.

Freddy stops and gets serious.

"You wanna help your dad?"

Travis, suddenly intensely interested, says:

"Yeaaaah."

"You wanna go to CyberWorld?" Freddy says, just as serious.

"Yeaaaah." Travis is even more interested.

"All we have to do is get to Vegas," says Freddy.

"**Vegas?** Did you take a stupid pill? How we gonna get to Vegas?" Travis shakes his head.

Freddy is stumped.

Travis is right.

Suddenly Freddy's eyes spot a flash of fool's gold reflecting off the credit card shimmy-shining in that shaft of sunlight showering through the window.

And with that, the final piece of the puzzle furiously fits together in Freddy's head, after which he says:

"We can use your old man's credit card, and—"

He never gets to finish that sentence.

"Are you out of you head?" says Travis.

"We'll be back before they even know we're gone, and—" says Freddy.

"No, no, no, no, no, no, no—" says Travis, shaking his head.

"Come on, man, don't be a child—" says Freddy.

"Shut up—" Travis shoots back.

"No, you shut up—" says Freddy.

"No, you shut up—" says Travis.

Freddy raises the stakes:

"Are you a man or a little boy?"

"What's that supposed to mean?" Travis demands.

"Man. Or little boy. Seems pretty clear to me." Freddy drips attitude. "A MAN solves problems. A little boy whines and cries about it. A MAN saves his family. A little boy sits at home and pouts. So which is it? A man or a little boy?"

"Now you're making me mad. You wanna see who's a man? I'll show you who's a man." Travis flies up the stairs, Freddy hounding his heels into the bedroom/sports emporium.

Travis picks up a baseball bat, swings it over his head, pauses, and smiles over at Freddy.

Travis brings the bat smashing down on his prized Bart Simpson bank, and it shatters into 151 pieces, unleashing $48.23 and sending little bits of shattered Bart scattering to the four corners of the room.

That's how serious he is.

Freddy grins from ear to ear.

"Ready, Freddy?" Travis smiles.

"Ready," says Freddy.

A Succubus, a Hair Ball & a Narrow Escape

he Walla Walla Airport is small for an airport, but Travis Best and Freddy Quigley don't know that. Because they've never been in an airport.

As they approach the counter, Freddy can feel his hands getting clammy as he whispers to Travis:

"You got your ID, right?"

"Yes," Travis hisses back. "For the squazillionth time, I got my ID."

Gene Grazinazzo stands behind a counter. The boys know his name is Gene because it says so on the name tag pinned to his hideous yellow jacket.

This is about the time in any plan where Freddy starts to get shaky. When other humans are involved, and they must be talked to.

Luckily, this is also the time when Travis shines.

"Can I help you boys?" Gene asks, with a jack-o'-lantern smile so wide it's terrifying.

Travis and Freddy flinch back from Gene Grazinazzo's high-voltage smile.

"Yes." Travis turns on his charm. "We'd like to buy two tickets to Las Vegas, please."

Freddy tries smiling, but he ends up looking somewhere between stupid and goofy.

"You kids want two tickets to Las Vegas?" Gene asks, talking loud and smiling hard, just in case his boss is watching.

"Yup," the boys say at the same time.

"And how are you kids gonna pay for that?" Gene asks, slightly thrown off by how perfectly together Travis and Freddy said "Yup."

"Gold card, my good man." Travis proudly hands Gene the card, like he's seen his dad do so many times.

"Sorry, kids, no can do," Gene says with a huge, almost demented smile, followed by a small fake frowny face to let the boys know that he feels bad about not taking their money and turning them into happy customers.

"Uh, we're meeting his father there. . . ." Travis says.

Unfortunately, Freddy picks the same moment to say:

"Yeah, uh, we're meeting his dad there. . . ."

An I'm-stupid-and-guilty look takes over Freddy's face.

An I-can't-believe-how-stupid-you-are look takes over Travis's face.

This is followed by an enormous, frightening smile from Gene.

"Sorry, kids, but you're too young to travel alone. But it sure has been a *real* pleasure serving you today."

Our heroes are crushed. Defeated at the first roadblock. If either had been alone, he would now have slunk home and sunk into a sad funk. Fortunately, they are together.

"Well, what do we do now, Boy Genius?" Travis spits out as they slink away.

"I don't think there's any need to be sarcastic . . . Succubus!" Freddy shoots back.

Travis thinks for a second, then says:

"*Succubus.* I like that. Define."

"It's a demon that assumes female form to suck the soul out of people," says Freddy.

"Cooooooool," says Travis. After a moment of thought, he says:

"The Raptor is a nasty succubus."

"Exactly," says Freddy.

Standing beside a bank of phones, these two almost-thirteen completely clueless boys desperately try to think as grown-up commuters buzz by.

"I got an idea," they say at exactly the same time.

"How could you possibly have an idea, your brain is too small," Freddy says, while at the same time Travis says:

"I'm sick and tired of your lame ideas, ya hairball!"

Together they say:

"What-ever!"

Freddy takes out his state-of-the-art iBrain mega-laptop Super Computer that Orange Computers sent to one hundred young international geniuses to test-drive.

Travis, clutching his dad's wallet, strides toward the security X-ray machine and yells:

"Dad! Dad!"

When Travis gets to the machine, he looks past it down the hall and says to the security guard:

"My dad forgot his wallet. I gotta get it to him."

Gus Goodyonson, security guard, an insomniac who hasn't had a good night's sleep in a year and a half, looks at the wallet, shrugs, and lets Travis walk through the X-ray machine.

"Dad, wait up!" Travis yells, like he really is trying to deliver the wallet to his dad.

He turns a corner, fist-pumps, and mouths:

"Yeeess!"

Travis finds the departures screen, locates the flight to Las Vegas, and walks to the gate, where fliers hand tickets to Flo Hope, the gate agent, before entering the tunnel that leads to the plane.

"Dad! Dad!" Travis yells again when he gets to Flo, looking really hard for his imaginary dad as he says to her:

"My dad forgot his wallet. I gotta get it to him."

Four months and three days earlier, Flo was fooled by

this exact scam and got into big trouble. As her boss bawled her out, she vowed:

I won't be fooled again.

"Give me his name," she says, "and I'll page him."

"Oh, that's okay, I don't mind." Travis smiles, trying to push his way down the tunnel.

"No trouble at all." Flo smiles back, stopping Travis with a stiff arm.

Unfortunately for her, at this exact moment, a couple of red-cheeked, cranky, colicky, cowlicky, two-month-old twins are strolled right into Flo Hope's knees.

The twins scream with double-barreled anger, bringing the airport to a standstill.

Travis waits a moment, then slips past the distracted Flo into the tunnel and walks right onto the plane.

"I'll show that little mollusk," Travis mutters happily, imagining Freddy's face when he hears that Travis's plan was the one that worked. Notice that even if Travis's stupid plan does work, he'll end up in Vegas by himself, without Freddy, and no way to get home. It should now be clear why Travis is not the brains of the outfit.

At that exact second, Freddy, who *is* the brains of the outfit, plugs into a computer-friendly pay phone with his iBrain mega-laptop while he mutters happily: "I'll show that mollusk."

It takes him twenty-seven seconds to hack into the airline's database, and another ninety-four seconds to input their information and get a confirmation code for two first-class round-trip tickets to Las Vegas, with these special instructions:

TO BE PICKED UP AT AIRPORT BY MINOR— UNACCOMPANIED TRAVEL APPROVED.

Freddy pushes the RETURN button on his iBrain megalaptop. It buzzes and hums, then finally, after what seems to Freddy like a large chunk of forever, one beautiful word appears on his screen.

APPROVED.

Freddy fist-pumps and mouths: "Yeessss!"

Then he walks to a counter, far away from Gene, and steps in front of Marsha Pringle. All she wants is for her horrible headache to take a vacation.

"I'm here to pick up two tickets to Las—"

Freddy's voice now decides to crack as it says: "Vegas!"

In a much higher register.

This does not help Marsha Pringle's headache.

Freddy turns stupid-red, his blood hots up, and his skin gets all sticky.

This is where Travis always steps in and saves the day.

But Travis, of course, is nowhere to be seen.

"Name?" Marsha says, flat as a Dutch pancake.

"Uh, my, uh," stammers Freddy, "the name is, uh, my father, George Best, if that's okay, and . . ."

If it had been almost any other clerk in the whole building, Freddy's pathetic performance would have gotten him busted, no ifs, ands, or buts.

But Marsha Pringle couldn't care less. Over the pounding in her own skull, she punches in the name, and this makes the computer snap, crackle, and pop.

Drops of hot sweat pop up like mushrooms on Freddy's forehead. Suddenly his shirt seems two sizes too small, and he can feel everybody staring at him, even though no one really is. His head gets tighter and tighter, and just as he sees it exploding, his big brain spraying all over Marsha Pringle, the first ticket miraculously starts sliding out of her computer.

Freddy's shoulders sag as sighs full of relief pour out of him, the tickets so close he can practically taste them.

"Could I see some ID, please?" asks Marsha.

Freddy's face looks like a clock that stopped ticking.

"ID? What? Uh, see the thing is—" When his voice decides to crack again on the word *is,* Freddy realizes he doesn't have any idea what the thing is.

As this is happening, Travis is sitting in seat 23C of an airplane headed to Las Vegas, furiously playing the game *Kill Baby Kill!* on his tiny PlayPocket game unit.

He's already killed forty-one aliens when Alice Flump, a flight attendant with gigantic scary hair, looms over him.

"Excuse me, young man, could I see your boarding pass?" asks a cranky Alice.

"Boarding pass?" asks a surprised Travis, who's sure he's home free and has let his guard down. "Yeah, sure, no problem."

He recovers and smiles a $750,000 smile.

But Alice Flump isn't buying any of it.

As Travis pretends to look in his pack, terror rides over his face. At times like this, Travis always wishes his brain was as big as Freddy's, because his own often acts like a broken CD player, turning beautiful music into ugly bits of random noise.

By the time he get his face out of his pack and shows it to Alice again, he's managed to work a $250,000 smile back on his face as he says:

"Oh yeah, I just remembered, my dad has it."

"And where is he?" asks Alice Flump.

"He's over there." Travis points vaguely with his great hair to nowhere in particular.

"Let's go talk to him," says Alice, the smell of fishiness thick around Travis.

"Oh, I just remembered, he's not actually on the plane," Travis says, realizing he's sounding more and more like a person telling a big fat lie and doing a very bad job of it.

"Could I see your boarding pass, please?" Alice asks again, hoping to take out her bad mood on Travis.

"Oh yeah, uh, I just remembered, my friend has it." Travis follows this very weak sentence with a smile owing several thousand dollars on it.

"You'd better come along with me, young man." Alice enjoys the look of panic pacing over Travis's handsome face.

Busted!

Travis imagines bitter disappointment twisting into his mom when she finds out what an idiotic stunt he's pulled. He's seen that look too many times in his life, and he's definitely not looking forward to seeing it again.

Alice grabs Travis's arm and pulls him down the aisle like he's a pitiful little kid.

Where's Freddy? is all his brain can think.

Down the tunnel and back into the airport Travis is yanked by Alice. She can't wait to take him straight to the airport authorities.

As Travis does an urgent search of the airport for Freddy, he feels the weight of failure climb on his shoulders and whisper in his ear:

"Travis, you are a clueless loser."

At that exact second, Freddy is pretending to frantically search his pack for some ID that'll prove he has something to do with Mr. George Best, while from the line behind him, an angry man shouts out:

"Little kiddies shouldn't be traveling without their mommies and daddies."

This makes Freddy look back at the angry man.

Naturally, when he does this, he sees Travis in the Raptor-like clutches of the mad Alice.

"Traaaaaaaaaaaaaaaaaavis!" Freddy yells.

"Fredddddddddddddddddy!" Travis yells.

Once again the airport stops dead for just a second, then comes back to life as passengers continue moving from point A to B to C all the way to Z.

"He's got my ID—" yells Freddy.

"He's got my ticket—" yells Travis.

In the confusion, Travis manages to unglue himself from the angry Alice.

When he gets to Freddy, he whispers: "You got the tickets?"

Freddy whispers back: "Gimme your ID."

Travis hands his ID to Freddy, who hands it to Marsha, who hands them the tickets.

Alice arrives, asking: "Does this boy have a ticket?"

"Yeah," says Marsha in a voice dripping with headache.

"Oh," says Alice in a voice rich with regret that she's not going to get to bust Travis.

Travis and Freddy do a tiny fist bump as they mouth: "YEESSSS!"

And so, tragedy becomes triumph, on its way to disaster.

A Swiped iBrain, Slim Slick Hicks & Sam the Cabby

WELCOME
TO *Las Vegas*

screams the sign under which Travis Best and Freddy Quigley wander, wide-eyed and wigging, as they're baddabing-baddaboomed by limo drivers, brushed aside by sick-rich sheikhs, ignored by bad singers with worse hair, growled at by business dudes who just lost their shirts, smacked by ticked-off retirees who like to whack twelve-year-old boys with their walkers, and trampled by a wild pack of bodybuilders going to a musclehead convention.

LAS VEGAS
Welcomes

Boom Boom   Bang Bang
MILLER   -   FARGAS

HEAVYWEIGHT
CHAMPIONSHIP BOUT

hangs on a banner.

The boys feel even smaller than they look.

In the Las Vegas Airport, one-armed-bandit slot machines stand along the walls like headless Transformers waiting to do battle.

Slim Slick Hicks, a thin zitty wiry guy, spots Travis Best and Freddy Quigley. His eyes go wide as he thinks: These kids are a lock. A solid lock.

Slim Slick Hicks just missed his flight to L.A., and even though he swore to his wife that he wouldn't steal anything in the airport, he just can't help himself.

So he walks up behind the boys real casual, snatches Freddy's bag full of iBrain mega-laptop, and power-walks away.

But as the boys stare, stunned and grim, while their chances of saving Trav's family and getting to Cyber-World for their thirteenth birthday disappear like smoke, Samantha "Sam" Phillips, a female cabby in a backwards Yankees cap, a beat-up leather bomber jacket, Manic Panic vampire-red lipstick, distressed red Chuck Taylor high-tops, ragged jeans, and a SHUT UP AND DANCE T-shirt, looks up just in time to see Slim Slick Hicks flee with the swiped iBrain while Freddy yells:

"STOP! THIEF!"

Everyone ignores his plea.

Everyone but Sam.

She takes two giant steps and sticks out a big red high-top, which trips Slim Slick Hicks, who flies butt over iBrain onto the airport floor.

In a flash, Sam puts her red high-top on Slim Slick's throat, and his face reds up, zits filling like little volcanoes about to explode out of his face.

Travis believes he's seeing things. So he looks away and shakes his head, expecting Slim Slick Hicks and Freddy's iBrain mega-laptop pack to be hightailing it out of the Vegas airport.

But when he looks back, Travis once again sees Sam's

red high-top pressing into the pustule-covered neck of Slim Slick Hicks, making lunch meat out of the creep who copped Freddy's bag.

Freddy's big brain, on the other hand, takes the whole thing in, and he says:

"WOW! Xena, Warrior Princess of Vegas."

The boys sprint to Sam.

At that exact second a one-armed bandit pays off, spitting up hundreds and hundreds of coins. The Vegas airport stops dead for just a second. Everyone stares at the winner while they think: I wish it was me winning all that free money. Then they resume moving from point A to B to C all the way to Z.

"Yo, Pumpkinhead," Sam barks at Slim Slick Hicks in a voice loaded with no-nonsense, "you're not tryin' to rip these kids off, are ya?"

"No way! This is my bag, lady," Slim Slick squeals, gasping for breath.

The amazing thing is how much it looks like he's telling the truth.

"That's **MY** bag!" says Freddy.

After which Travis says:

"His **iBrain mega-laptop** is in it!"

"It's got my **name** on it," Freddy says.

"**Yeah!**" Travis adds.

Having a red Chuck Taylor high-top pushed into your throat while you're lying on an airport floor clutching freshly stolen goods generally makes a person do whatever the red high-top wearer wants you to.

So when Sam reaches down for the bag, Slim Slick Hicks has little choice but to let her have it.

Sure enough, on a little tag, it says:

FREDDY QUIGLEY

"Are you Freddy Quigley?" Sam asks Travis.

"No, **he** is," Travis says, pointing.

As Freddy says: "Yeah, **I** am!"

Slim Slick now figures the only thing to do is squirm his way out of it. Luckily, he's a world-class squirmer.

"Oh, will ya look at that," he croaks. "I have a bag exactly like this. Sorry, kid, real sorry, you know, I—"

Sam pushes down on Slick Hick's throat a little harder, and the words choke to a stop.

"Try pickin' on somebody your own size next time!" Sam leans into Slim Slick when she says this so he knows how serious she is.

She removes her shoe from his windpipe.

This is one scary chick, Slim Slick Hicks thinks as his eyes bug and he says with a small, knowing grin:

"Hey, my apologies—honest mistake."

Gasping for air, he jumps to his wiry feet. Then, like a worm wriggling off a hook, he disappears with a quick juke n' jive into the crowd.

Sam, holding Freddy's precious mega-gigabyte cargo, turns to the boys and says:

"You boys lose somethin'?"

"Yeah, thanks!" says Freddy.

"That was wicked cool," says Travis.

"Out-standing!" says Freddy.

As she sizes up these two young hayseeds, Sam smiles. She doesn't smile often, but when she does, it lights up any joint.

"Where you two from?" she asks.

"Walla Walla, Washington," they reply at the same time.

Sam laughs, and as she holds up Freddy's bag she says:

"You're not in Walla Walla anymore, boys."

Freddy grabs the bag.

Only Sam doesn't let go.

So now they're both holding Freddy's bag full of iBrain mega-laptop together.

Sam looks hard into Freddy's eyes, then hard into Travis's eyes. Then she says:

"You two be careful, you hear me?"

Together they say:

"Yes, ma'am."

Sam smiles again and then lets go, and suddenly Freddy's got his bag back.

"Where you boys headed?" she asks, switching into Sam the Cabby mode.

This question takes the boys by surprise. In all the excitement, they have forgotten this one small detail.

Luckily, Freddy's big brain starts working overtime, while Travis's big mouth does the same.

"Uh, well, the thing is, we're headed to, you know—"

Freddy's search engine finally gets a hit, and he says:

"A hotel!"

"Yeah, a hotel." Travis smoothes everything out with that smile, like he's done so many times before.

"Sounds like you boys need a cab," says Sam.

Together they say:

"Definitely!"

As they climb into Sam's cab, they have no idea that they are zooming toward their date with the huge scary men who will dangle them in their underpants.

Lost Wages, Binary Polynomials & the Hoosegow

Sam likes to drive fast. Which is good when you're a cabdriver. Unless you crash into stuff. Like other cars. Or people. Luckily, Sam almost never does this. She careens, tires squealing, asphalt screaming, out of the airport, Travis Best and Freddy Quigley slamming back in their seats as Sam zips, zigs, and zags through the neon lights that are the Strip.

I'd never drive this fast, thinks Freddy.

I can't wait to drive this fast, thinks Travis.

"So what brings you boys to Lost Wages?" asks Sam.

"You mean Las Vegas," says Freddy.

Sam rolls her eyes.

"Lost Wages . . . Las Vegas, get it, doi-boy?" says Travis.

"Oh . . ." says Freddy sheepishly. "Good one."

"We're goin' to a math thing." Travis nods like he actually knows what he's talking about. "Freddy here's giving a big talk."

"I am?" Freddy asks quietly.

Travis elbows him. Freddy gets it.

"Actually, I'm presenting a paper on the implications of Ribbet's work on the Riemann hypothesis," Freddy's big brain churns out.

"Oh yeah, ribbets an' Riemann's," Travis says, trying to camouflage his smaller, slower brain.

Sam is not easily impressed, so when she stares at the boys in the rearview mirror with an impressed look on her face, it really means something.

"So what do you do when you're not driving a cab?" Freddy asks.

"I'm the mayor," Sam says with the straightest of faces.

"Really?" the boys ask together.

"Yeah, really," Sam cracks back with extreme sarcasm so the boys know she's not really the mayor of Las Vegas, and that they're a couple of young dorks for thinking she is.

"Good one," they say.

"He's Freddy," says Travis.

"And he's Travis," says Freddy.

"Sam," says Sam.

"Hi, Sam," Travis and Freddy say.

"Hello, Travis and Freddy," says Sam.

"So, how's it goin'?" asks Travis.

"Uh, not good," says Sam.

"How come?" asks Freddy.

"Actually, I'm—" She stops. Clearly, she wants to unburden, but needs some encouragement.

"What . . . what is it?" asks Travis with genuine interest.

Because they're so un-Vegas, Sam feels strangely relaxed around Travis and Freddy. Who are they gonna talk to? she thinks. If I can't tell them, who can I tell?

"Well," she says, "if you really wanna know, I'm tryin' to get my dad outta the hoosegow."

Travis and Freddy look at each other. They know all about old-man trouble, but they have no idea what a hoosegow is. So Travis asks:

"What's a hosecow?"

"The hoosegow, the slammer, the pokey, lights-out, the Big Rock," says Sam.

Travis and Freddy shake their heads, indicating that they still have no idea what she's talking about.

"Prison!" Sam says.

"Your dad's in prison?" Travis asks, eyes widening as he sees himself visiting his dad in jail, talking into that little telephone through the Plexiglas.

"Yeah," says Sam.

"Really sorry," say Travis and Freddy.

"Yeah, he got set up by this schmuck Johnny Large, maybe you heard of him—" Sam cuts a limo off, then whiplashes breakneck around a corner.

"Who's he?" says Travis. He immediately regrets it,

because he knows his very best friend is gonna make some wise-aleck crack about how stupid he is, and if he'd just kept his mouth shut, Freddy woulda just said who the guy was, and that woulda been that. The thing about keeping your mouth shut, Travis thinks, is that it's often such a good idea, and yet it's so hard to do.

"You'll have to excuse my friend," says Freddy. "He has small rocks in his head where a brain should be. Johnny Large is the King of Vegas, which is ironic because he's a small rotund man."

"*Rotund* means round and plump," says Travis proudly.

"Thank you," says Sam.

"My pleasure." Travis smiles.

"So what happened?" Freddy asks Sam.

"Some shady business came down," Sam seethes, "and my old man got set up and shafted by Johnny Large."

"That sucks," says Travis.

"Sucks big-time," says Freddy.

"You ain't lying," says Sam, liking these kids more and more. "But I'm gonna clear his name and get my old man outta jail, and I'm gonna nail Johnny Large, if it's the last thing I do, and that's a fact, Jack."

"Viva Las Vegas," as sung by the Elvis Presley, suddenly blasts on the radio, and Sam cranks it, seat-dancing while she cruises with gleeful speed.

"Viva Las Vegas," she screams.

So Travis and Freddy scream:

"Viva Las Vegas!"

When the song's over, they all crack up laughing.

Feels good to laugh, Sam thinks as she says:

"Ahhhhh, the King!"

Travis and Freddy, not wanting to be uncool, repeat:

"Ahhhh, the King."

Travis and Freddy have no idea who Elvis Presley is yet, or that he's the King to whom Sam is now referring.

The glamorous, glimmery, glowwormy neon of Las Vegas looks like Christmas, the Fourth of July, and being a millionaire all rolled into one. Travis and Freddy stick their heads out the window like moonstruck dogs, mouths agape at this gaudy jewel of the desert, while howling:

"Wooooooooooooooooooow!"

"You palookas never been to Vegas?" Sam asks.

"We've never been outta Walla Walla," say Travis and Freddy.

"Well, you should get a kick out of this hotel; it's a serious spectacle," says Sam.

"Thanks, we really appreciate this," says Freddy.

"Yeah, thanks," chimes in Travis.

"Remember, there's a lotta scumbuckets out there, so keep yer eyes peeled and yer noses clean."

Sam squeals to a halt in front of the Excalibur Hotel

& Casino, turns around, leans over the seat, and with her face right in theirs, she says:

"Understand?"

"Yes, ma'am," say Travis and Freddy.

And even though they plan on getting their noses plenty dirty, they look like they mean it.

Travis and Freddy step onto the sizzling Vegas sidewalk, under the huge blinking Excalibur sign that flashes:

BOOM BANG
BOOM BANG
MILLER - FARGAS

HEAVYWEIGHT
CHAMPIONSHIP BOUT

"You two bad boys take it easy," says Sam.

"Yeah, hey, thanks, seriously, really—"

"Hey, yeah, thanks, really, seriously—"

Travis and Freddy say over each other.

Carl Sears, a loose-jointed man in a loose-fitting suit with a nose that's been broken three times and a heart that's been broken once, saunters by the boys.

When Carl sees Sam, his face lights up.

When Sam sees Carl, her face goes dark.

"Oh, is the Village Idiot Convention in town?" Sam snarls at Carl.

"You're beautiful when you're mean." Carl grins at Sam, the woman who broke his heart.

"I was having such a good day till you showed up," Sam shoots back.

"I do what I can," Carl shoots back.

"Obviously, it's not enough," adds Sam.

Travis and Freddy smile wide, following the Carl–Sam banter like they're watching a tennis match.

"By the way, your conscience called, it's at lost and found, and apparently no one wants to claim it." Sam smirks with a chuckle.

Travis and Freddy nod in appreciation.

"Ooooooooooooooooooooooh! Good one!"

Sam does a mini-bow for the boys.

"And who are these two chuckleheads?" asks Carl.

"Travis and Freddy, outta Walla Walla, Washington," says Sam.

Travis and Freddy nod. "Nice to meet you."

"Is he your boyfriend?" asks Freddy.

"In his dreams," says Sam.

"In my dreams, you're as sweet as the first day I laid eyes on you," Carl says into Sam's eyes. Then he turns to the boys and says:

"Nice meeting you, fellas."

After Carl slides away, Sam says:

"That's the guy who helped put my old man away."

"Ouch . . ." says Travis.

"Sorry . . ." says Freddy.

"Yup." Sam sighs, then says: "Later, boys!"

Then she hops in her cab as the boys say:

"Thanks, Sam!"

After she fishtails away in a blaze of burning rubber, Travis says:

"She is way cool."

"Cool to the google," says Freddy.

Travis and Freddy look up and shake their heads in awe.

From the thirty-fifth floor of the Excalibur Hotel, they look like teeny tiny boy specks in the vast Vegas afternoon.

In less than twenty-four hours, that's what they'll look like if you stare up from this exact spot, except they'll be dangling in their tighty-whities.

Pickles, Feathers & a Rubber Chicken

ravis Best and Freddy Quigley have never been inside a hotel, much less a Las Vegas hotel, so they have no idea that the Excalibur is odd, even by Vegas standards.

It's extra odd because the entire Excalibur staff wears costumes of characters from the age of King Arthur and Camelot.

A King Arthur is currently struggling with the over-stuffed luggage of a stout old lady dragging a miniature monster Shih Tzu. They both yap in high hideous yelping yips.

Travis and Freddy step up to the counter so they can check in with a man dressed in a huge floppy hat, pointy shoes, green tights, and a ruffled shirt with a name tag that reads:

SIR GALAHAD

"Prithee, young weary travelers, how may I assist thee?" says Tony "Pickles" Piccioni, a guy pretending in the lamest way to be Sir Galahad.

Pickles hates his floppy hat. He hates his pointy shoes. He hates his ruffled shirt. But most of all he hates his green tights. What he really wants is to be a Scary Gangster. He believes he has the necessary tools and temperament. He just doesn't know how to get started. But he does know for a fact that no Scary Gangster would be caught dead in these cheesy green tights.

"What?" say Travis and Freddy, confused.

"Huzzah, sirrahs, may I servest thee?" Pickles rolls his eyes, showing how little of his heart he's putting into pretending to be Sir Galahad.

"Uh, what?" Travis and Freddy mumble.

Pickles leans in and talks low so his boss won't hear. "What do you kids want?"

"We wanna check in," Travis whispers back, figuring this is the way things are done in hotels.

Pickles sees his boss walking by, so he says real loud: "Huzzah! Hast thou a reservation?"

"Oh yeah." Travis smiles.

"Uh, no." Freddy frowns a second later.

"But here's my father's credit card—" Freddy starts.

"He's meeting us here later," Travis finishes.

"And prithee, where be thy pater?" Pickles tries not to sound as annoyed as he is.

"What?" ask Travis and Freddy.

"Where's your old man?" Pickles whispers.

"He's coming, you know, uh . . ." Travis starts.

"Later," Freddy finishes.

"Upon the return of thy pater, I shall talk to thee anon," Pickles says loudly, trying to smile at his boss but doing a very bad job of it.

Travis and Freddy have no idea what he's talking about and try not to show the panic that's creeping like slime-trailing slugs down their throats.

Tony leans in again and whispers:

"Can't check in without your old man."

Travis starts to say something.

Then he stops and shuts his mouth, remembering how good it can be to keep your mouth shut.

He and Freddy shuffle away, their crests fully fallen.

Brian Feathers, a porter dressed as a Court Jester in multi-motley-colored tights and a pointy hat with dangling jingly bells, carrying a rubber chicken, walks up to Pickles (whom he hates for no apparent reason), crosses his eyes comically, and proclaims in a silly high-pitched voice:

"A slap for luck!"

Then he slaps Pickles in the side of the head with the rubber chicken.

When the rubber chicken hits Pickles, he flips, leaps over the counter like a wild animal, and starts pummeling the rubber-chicken-wielding Court Jester.

In fairness to Pickles, this is the sixth time Brian has whacked him in the last three days, and in fact Brian has already been warned by his supervisor to cease and desist all further chicken-slapping behavior.

Travis Best and Freddy Quigley see none of this, as they're headed away from the check-in desk toward a bank of pay phones, fighting the terrible feeling that their already shaky ship has sprung a leak and is going to leave them buried in a hole in the bottom of the sea.

Freddy jacks his laptop into a pay phone and tries to slither undetected into the Excalibur system. After much button pushing and muttering, these dreaded words flash on his screen:

ACCESS DENIED

Over and over, Freddy is stymied.

ACCESS DENIED
ACCESS DENIED
ACCESS DENIED
ACCESS DENIED
ACCESS DENIED
ACCESS DENIED
ACCESS DENIED
ACCESS DENIED

ACCESS DENIED
ACCESS DENIED
ACCESS DENIED

Travis is shocked. He was sure Freddy could get into anything, anywhere, anytime.

"What's going on?" he asks in panic.

"I don't know. . . ." Freddy growls in panic.

Just when they're about to throw in the imaginary towel that would signal their utter failure and defeat, Freddy sees something he hopes will make everything better and heads toward a bank of elevators.

Travis follows. He's seen this look before. The boy genius has an Idea.

An elevator opens, but when Travis starts to enter with the other passengers, Freddy stops him.

Thirty-five seconds later another elevator opens and empties. As the elevator's mouth starts to close, Freddy hops in. Travis stands there with a blank stare until Freddy pulls him into the elevator and pushes the button for the thirty-fifth floor.

As they pass the seventh floor, Freddy pushes the EMERGENCY STOP button, and the elevator grinds to a halt with a shudder.

"Hey, what are you doing?" Travis demands.

Freddy jacks his laptop into the emergency elevator telephone.

"And Freddy Quigley, the Gigabyte Kid, shows once again why he's such a crowd favorite here in Lost Wages!"

Freddy makes the sound of a cheering crowd as he hooks the wires together.

Travis watches in amazement.

It takes Freddy twenty-one seconds to tap into the Excalibur reservation system.

Unfortunately, there's no room at the inn.

Freddy scans floor after floor after floor.

Nothing. Nada. Nil. Zilch. Zip. Zero.

Suddenly a voice full of gravel rattles over the intercom:

"This is security. Is everyone all right?"

Travis and Freddy trade scared faces.

"Hello?" Travis tries to fill the elevator intercom with charm.

"What seems to be the problem?" Security Guy's voice pounds through the speaker.

"No problem, we're cool, we're good, we're excellent," Travis riffs as Freddy frantically searches for a room, with absolutely no success.

"Hang tight, I'm sending somebody right up there," booms the bodiless voice.

"No, that's okay, everything's totally . . . uh, you know . . . cool." Try as he might, Travis can't stop sounding as frazzled and freaked as he feels.

And Freddy still can't find a vacancy.

"We going to manual operation," says the hidden crackling voice. "We'll have you out of there in no time."

"No, that's okay, we don't mind, really." Travis is officially starting to Lose It.

The elevator shakes and rumbles to life like Frankenstein's monster.

"Hurry up, Freddy," Travis frantically whispers.

Just as they're reaching the ground floor, Freddy spots a vacancy on the thirty-fifth floor.

"Bingo! The Elvis Suite—"

Travis:

"Take it."

"Okay," says Freddy, fingers flying.

Suddenly the elevator touches down on the ground floor, and the doors are about to slide open with Freddy and his beloved iBrain still jacked into the elevator phone.

Busted!

Travis deflates, and thinks: Mom is gonna kill me.

Freddy's working too hard to think anything.

The elevator doors slowly part, revealing Security Guy, with a head the size and density of a medicine ball.

Travis tries to smile, all set to launch into a wild story involving Pakistan pocket rockets and a Shetland pony, when he notices that Security Guy is *not* staring at them like they're hacking into the hotel computer system.

When Travis turns around, he sees that Freddy has miraculously stuffed his iBrain back into his bag.

"Everything okay?" booms Security Guy.

"Ohhhhh, yeah!" Travis and Freddy simultaneously say.

They have no idea how wrong they are.

A Heart Attack, a Hound Dog & a Little Debbie

n the Elvis Suite, it's all Elvis all the time: Elvis nightlights, Elvis toothbrushes, an Elvis clock with legs that swing with every second, Elvis ashtrays, a singing Elvis toilet seat, and Elvis painted on velvet playing poker with four dogs: a French poodle, a bulldog, a Great Dane, and a hound dog, while "Hound Dog" plays in the background.

Travis Best and Freddy Quigley still have no idea who Elvis is.

A knock knocks on the door.

Travis and Freddy jump out of their overstuffed chairs. They are happy as hungry cats dropped into a room full of fat blind mice.

Two words can explain the glee of Travis and Freddy.

Room.

Service.

They roar toward the door, their spit glands flash-flooding as the big TV plays *When Wild Animals Kill Each Other*.

Together they yell.

"Rooooooooom ser-vice!!!"

When Travis and Freddy open the door, their knees weaken, and their tummies rumble like thunder.

Room Service Guy rolls in the cart.

If Travis and Freddy had been paying attention, they would have noticed that this Room Service Guy looks very familiar, despite the fact that he's wearing a huge feathery hat, pointy shoes, green tights, and a ruffled shirt.

But Travis and Freddy are too busy ogling their feast to notice anything.

"Double fudge brownies—" says Travis.

"Check—" says Freddy.

"Chocolate layer cake—" Travis.

"Check—" Freddy.

"Hot fudge sundaes—" Travis.

"Check—" Freddy.

"Hot chocolate with extra whipped cream—" Travis.

"Check—" Freddy.

"Cruller, bear claw, glazed, powdered, sprinkled, and jelly-filled—" Travis.

"Check—" Freddy.

"Devil Dogs, Ho Hos, Little Debbies—" Travis.

"Check—" Freddy.

"One liter Dr Pepper, one liter root beer—" Travis.

"Check, check—" Freddy.

They survey their bountiful booty like plundering

pirates, then chest-bump fist-bump, snap fingers into six-shooters and blow away the smoke.

Room Service Guy smiles, while wondering, What are these boys doing unsupervised in the Elvis Suite in Las Vegas?

Suddenly the boys realize he's studying them.

As Freddy's big brain searches for a clue what to do, Travis stares at Room Service Guy, thinking, Where have I seen this dude before? Then he motions ever so slightly for Freddy to study him. Which Freddy does.

Result: instant recognition.

"Hey," says Freddy, "you're that guy who's hot fer Sam."

"Oh, man," says Travis, "you look like the King of Dorks."

Freddy laughs. "Good one."

"Guilty as charged," says Carl.

"Did you use to be her boyfriend?" asks Travis.

"Sam, that is," clarifies Freddy.

"Well . . . maybe you should ask her about that," says Carl.

"Did you really get her old man sent to the house-goo?" Travis asks.

"The what?" asks Carl.

"The poker—" says Freddy.

"What are you guys talkin' about?" asks Carl.

"She said you helped send her old man to jail," says Travis.

Carl knows that's what she thinks, but when he hears it, it hits him like a hard punch to the heart.

"Did you?" Freddy asks in his small voice.

"No"—Carl sighs sadly—"but . . . I can see how she thinks that. It was Johnny Large. I was after him, but he's . . . a very clever, evil guy, and there was nothing I could do about it."

"Really?" say Travis and Freddy.

"Really," says Carl with a sad shake of head.

A wounded silence hangs heavy over Travis, Freddy, Carl, and all that room-service food. It's the kind of silence that makes you want to say something, only you can't think of the right thing to say, as your throat closes and your chest hurts and your mouth goes all dry.

Finally Travis says:

"Hey, Carl, you want somethin' to eat?"

"Yeah, man, help yourself to . . . whatever," says Freddy.

"No thanks." Carl smiles. "But lemme explain how it works: I bring the food, you give me a tip, then I leave."

"Oh right, tip—" Freddy hits his flat palm on his large forehead.

WAP!

"Tip, sure, the tip," adds Travis.

"Doi," they say together.

Travis goes on a fishing expedition into the pond of his pocket and nets forty-seven cents in pennies, nickels, and dimes.

As Travis hands Carl the coinage, Carl shakes his head and says:

"No."

"No?" the boys ask.

"Can't give people coins," explains Carl. "It's an insult."

"Wow." Travis and Freddy are boggled that anyone would be insulted by receiving coin money when they've spent so much of their lives hunting for it.

Freddy hands Carl a crumpled-up five-dollar bill.

Carl shakes his chuckling head and hands it back.

"No."

"No?" the boys ask.

"Make it real casual," says Carl. "Like this."

He shakes Travis's hand, secretly leaving a five-dollar bill there without Freddy even knowing, while saying:

"Thanks, my man."

Travis waves the five at Freddy and says:

"Did you see that, man? That was sooooo cool."

"Mad cool," says Freddy.

"Lemme try that," says Travis.

He shakes Carl's hand and palms him the five while he smiles and says:

"Thanks, my man."

Carl looks at the five, shakes his head, and says:

"Not bad."

"Okay, lemme try," says Freddy.

He palms the five, reaches it out to Carl, and says:

"Thanks, my man."

Unfortunately, being Freddy, he lets go of the bill too soon, and it flutters dumbly to the rug.

Travis rolls his eyes and says:

"Smooth move, Ex-Lax."

Carl chuckles.

"Sorry," says Freddy.

"It's the thought that counts," says Carl, who slides the fiver into his pocket.

Carl eyeballs the boys hard, and says:

"Who you fellas here with?"

"We're here with his dad." Travis points at Freddy, who points back at Travis.

"Whose dad?" Carl's eyes narrow as his suspicion rises.

"Both of our dads, we're twins—you know, those twins that don't look alike," says Travis.

Freddy nods. "Fraternal twins."

"With different mothers," adds Travis.

"Right," finishes Freddy.

Carl knows there's something off about these boys, but try as he might, he can't quite finger it.

"I'm warning you," Carl says severely. "There are

some evil dudes out there. If there's anything you need, call room service and ask for Carl. You got that?"

"Got it," say Travis and Freddy.

"Any questions?" Carl says, very serious.

"Well, actually, there is one thing," says Travis.

"Yeah?" says Carl.

"Who's this guy Elvis?" asks Travis.

Carl laughs, then says:

"You guys are droll on a roll."

"Good one," say Travis and Freddy.

Carl smiles and leaves.

Travis and Freddy, alone finally with all that fabulous food, look at each other in awe, look back at the magical feast, then shout:

"Roooooooooooooom Serviiiiiiiiiiiiiiice!"

Freddy swan-dives with a spoon headfirst into the brownies while Travis cannonballs into the hot fudge sundae.

As they gorge on their gorgeous gooey goodies, they make a sound like this:

"Aaaaaaaarghohhhhhhhmmmmmmyeahhhhhhh-hhwowwwuhuhhuhuhhuhwhoooooooooooo."

As they work their way through the wonderland of whipped cream, the mountains of mind-boggling munchies, and the loverly layers of luscious cake, Freddy watches the blackjack video *How to Win in Vegas* over and over and over and over and over and over, until his big brain has swallowed, digested, and memorized the whole thing frontwards and backwards.

Quietly, Travis takes out his homemade slingshot, puts a maraschino cherry covered in whipped cream in the soft leather pocket, and pulls the rubber band back until it's stretched tight, full of dynamic and dramatic tension.

Silently, he lines Freddy's head up in his sights.

With a *whoosh* he lets the cherry fly.

It strafes straight at Freddy's bad haircut, traveling sixty-nine miles an hour, four mph over the speed limit for a cherry.

Freddy, elbow-deep in Ho Hos, is blissfully unaware that a cherry comet is slamming straight at his head.

The cherry explodes in a merry red mess onto the side of Freddy's head, his glasses flying, and his mouth yowling:

"OWWWW!"

This is followed by the sound of Travis laughing as loud as he's ever laughed in his life.

It sounds like this:

"HAAAAAAHAHAHA! HAAAAAAHAHAHA! HAAAAAAHAHAHA!"

For a split second, with all that red flying by his eye, Freddy thinks he's been shot.

Only when Freddy hears Travis laughing does he realize that he's fine, and that he's been used once again. As a butt. Of a Travis Best joke.

"You think that's funny?" asks Freddy, even though it's clear that Travis thinks it is, in fact, howlingly funny.

"Yeah, I do," Travis manages to squeeze through the laughs.

Freddy turns a giant serving spoon into a catapult by loading it up with whipped cream, cocking and aiming it right at Travis.

"How about this? You think this is funny?" Freddy's been trying his whole life to stick up for himself. Seems like a good time to start.

Travis stops laughing and slides into his oh-so-serious voice.

"Don't even think about it."

"Or what? Whatta ya gonna do?" Freddy grins, the ladled whipped cream ready to launch at Travis.

"Or you're gonna be very sorry, that's what," Travis hisses through gritted teeth.

"Ooooooooooooooooohhh, I'm soooooooooooo scared," Freddy says as he pretends to shake in his imaginary boots.

"I'm warnin' you." Travis eases slowly toward Freddy.

"Take another step, and I let her rip." Freddy's not sure whether he really means it or not.

"You wouldn't dare," says Travis, sure Freddy doesn't mean it.

"Ulcerated tumor—" says Freddy.

"Blood clot—" says Travis.

"Polyp—" says Freddy.

With his best, I'm-the-boss-of-you 'tude, Travis takes one big step toward Freddy.

With his best you're-not-the-boss-of-me 'tude, Freddy flings forward his spoon, and a fluffy white cloud of whipped cream screams straight toward Travis.

Travis was not expecting this, and by the time he realizes that Freddy has actually launched the whipped cream, it's way too late.

A white plume plops on top of Travis's head, followed by a giant glorp kersplatting on his barely closed right eye, up his open left nostril, across his shocked lips, and down his stunned chin.

Direct hit.

Now it's Freddy's turn to laugh:

"HARHARHAR SNORT

HARHARHAR SNORT
HARHARHAR SNORT!"

Travis checks himself in the mirror, and even he has to laugh at the cream-colored loon staring back at him.

When they're done laughing, Travis and Freddy look at each other, and at exactly the same time they scream:

"FOOOOOOOOOOD
FIIIIIIIIIIIIIIIIGHT!"

Gobs of goo, nougat of nutty loveliness, and chunks of fudge-dunked yumminess, along with the odd Ho Ho and the occasional Little Debbie, fly around the Elvis Suite like they haven't since the King himself stayed there toward the fat end of his life.

Seventeen minutes later, when it's all over, Travis and Freddy, along with many Elvis objects, are drenched with dessert products, and they proceed to eat themselves stupid sugar sick.

A Thump, a Loogey & a Snoogy Pigeon

HUMPTHUMPTHUMP.

Travis and Freddy lift their heads at exactly the same time, tumbled from slumber by the dull thud coming from the other side of the door.

When they both moan, it sounds like this:

"Awwwwnngggnnmmmawwowww."

Their stomachs rumble with trouble.

Their brains ache with pain.

Their throats are coated with sugary milky loogey goo.

THUMPTHUMPTHUMP.

Travis and Freddy stare, terrified, at the door.

They stare at each other, smothered under the mother of all sugar hangovers.

"Somebody's at the door," whispers Freddy in a croak-choked voice. There isn't just a frog in his throat, it's a whole Gila monster. He can't wait to hack up the huge phlegm ball that's hanging out in his gullet, courtesy of all that cake, whipped and ice cream.

"Doi," bleats Travis, who's looking forward to hacking and hocking a major-league loogey of his own.

Travis and Freddy look around at the cakey catastrophe that is their room.

The Elvis Suite doesn't look so nice covered with soiled sweets.

THUMPTHUMPTHUMP.

The boys are hoping the thumping goes away.

THUMPTHUMPTHUMP.

Doesn't sound like that's gonna happen anytime soon.

"Answer the door," Freddy whispers through the snoog overcoat his throat is wearing.

"You answer the door," whispers Travis, sick and stupefied.

When it's clear neither is going alone, they stumble to the door together.

"All Shook Up" plays as they crack the door open and peek out through slitted peepers.

It's Carl, in his huge feathery hat, green tights, and ruffled shirt.

"You fellas behavin' yerselves?" He smiles.

"What?" Travis and Freddy can barely hear above the sound of their head-banging sugar hangovers.

"Your dad here yet?" asks Carl, louder.

"No, he's gambling—" says Travis.

Unfortunately, at the same time, Freddy says:

"No, he's golfing."

Then Travis says:

"He's golfing."

At the same time Freddy says:

"He's gambling."

They look at each other and shut up.

This allows Travis to take over:

"Actually, he's golfing *and* gambling."

"He likes to gamble on golfing," says Freddy.

All this talking makes their heads hurt, while the huge loogies scream from their throats:

"Get me outta here!"

"I see." Carl isn't buying any of it.

"Carl," Travis asks in his Little Kid voice.

"Yeah," Carl answers, trying to help the kids come clean with whatever it is they're trying to come clean with.

"Let's suppose somebody made kind of a mess in their hotel room—" starts Travis.

"Or let's suppose they made kind of a big mess, and, uh . . ." Freddy tries to finish, but can't.

"How big a mess?" asks Carl.

Travis and Freddy inch open the door a little more.

Carl pokes his head in as far as he can and whistles low as he thinks: Looks like Ben & Jerry barfed in there.

"Don't worry, I'll take care of it," he says.

Travis and Freddy expel a deep warm sigh.

"You want some money?" Freddy asks, while Travis makes a thank-you face and says:

"Yeah, we could give you some money."

"No," says Carl, "this one's on the house. You boys clear out. I'll be back in about half an hour."

"Thanks, man." The boys quiver quietly as Carl takes off.

It's hard to say whether the boys look or feel worse. They try to clear their throats, but there's just too much sugary milky muck in there.

Travis slides open the glass door, and Freddy follows him out onto the balcony.

There they hack up the hugest snoog-goo-loogey hairball they've ever hacked, pulling up load after load, with great guttural retches that sound like this:

"Ughhhglurrrphhckkkachhuhhh."

The boys look at each other, heads tilted back, and nod. Game on!

Travis and Freddy take a running start, and as they reach the railing of the balcony, they spit, expectorating two huge hockers.

The majestic milky missiles soar in slow motion, their yellowy beigey greeny bilious bulk zooming off the Elvis

Suite balcony, hanging there in midair, then slowly plummeting, like lung-cookie smart bombs.

The twin projectiles nose-dive in full plunge.

Down.

Down.

Down.

Freddy's hits first:

KERSPLAT!

The sploogy fusillade explodes on the head of an unsuspecting pigeon, which staggers, stunned under the weight.

Two-point-four seconds later the other lactose salvo slams into the tail feathers of said pigeon, which stands like a statue soaked in human goo.

Travis and Freddy fist-bump, smiling as the fog of milk-shake-hot-fudge-layer-cake hangover begins to lift.

Binky, Vlurpa & Moose

ook at all that money. Silvery coins and sweet green bills, sliding into slots, morphing into chips, spit out of ATMs, slipped out of billfolds, converted and carted away in huge tubs to be counted, moved, and spent by men like Johnny Large.

Travis, drunk from all that money, suddenly realizes he's standing at the edge of the casino with his mouth hanging open like the loser doofus of the universe.

Travis glances at Freddy, whose mouth also hangs open like he's the loser doofus of the universe.

"Dude, don't go all dorkus on me." Travis nudges Freddy, who shuts his trap pronto.

The casino floor flashes with pulsating neon, beeping, ding-ding-dinging, alive with the buzz of excited maniacal people, almost all of whom are in the process of losing money.

The dealers are dressed like chain-shirted, fake-armored Knights.

The waitresses are dressed like Wenches, in flouncy

blouses and swishing skirts with peacock-eye rhine-stones glittering.

The bouncers are in black hoods and robes, like hungry-for-blood Executioners.

"Smile," says Travis, smiling so Freddy can see what a real smile is supposed to look like.

Freddy tries to whip out a similar smile, but alas, his is all teeth and braces.

Travis rolls his eyes and leads them in.

Ralph "Binky" Binkleman stands behind a window turning money into chips, dressed in a huge feathery hat, pointy shoes, cheesy green tights, and a ruffled shirt.

Binky likes wearing tights. They make him feel happy for some reason he can't entirely explain.

"We'd like to buy $38.14 worth of chips," says Travis, smiling like he has no idea that only a first-class moron would say something like that.

"Whatta ya, a couple of wise guys?" asks Binky as he smoothes out his tights lovingly.

"No." Travis and Freddy are very sincere.

"Well then, youze two are just stupid," says Binky, who has hardly any friends, mainly because he likes to tell people how stupid they are. "Everybody knows little kids can't bet. Come back in about ten years, though, 'cuz we really like stupid people here."

Binky feels very good about his blistering quip and looks around to see if anyone's watching so they'll see how smart he is.

Sadly for him, no one is.

Travis and Freddy slink away, sinking under the weight of their own stupidity.

Now, at last, just when Travis and Freddy believe all is lost, they meet the villainous yet tiny brute who's going to teach them what loss is really all about.

The front doors fly open. The sun blasts in with millionaire extraordinaire Johnny Large, all 5'2" of him, orbited by supermodels Vlurpa and KiKiKi, and his musclemen, Moose and No Neck.

Everybody stares, whispers, and points, buzzing and swarming around Johnny Large, as if by touching the hem of his $10,000 suit, some of his fortune will rub off on them.

Johnny Large smiles and waves like he owns the world.

Which in Vegas, he pretty much does.

Naturally, Travis and Freddy are totally unaware he's there, too lost in the depths of their own gloom and doom to notice the gloom and doom right behind them.

Until suddenly our almost thirteen-year-old heroes are blocking the path of Johnny Large and his entourage.

Travis and Freddy feel the hugeness of the tiny Mr. Large in back of them, and a spooky shudder shimmies up their spines.

Slooooooooowly, they turn.

Notice how the lights reflect off the shiny silver suit, shiny silver shirt, and shiny silver shoes of wee Johnny Large.

"That's Johnny Large," whispers Freddy.

"Doi," Travis whispers back.

Eyes agog, the boys stare, mouths hanging slack.

"Ya catch flies like that, boys," quips little Mr. Large.

The deafening laughs that splash up from Vlurpa, KiKiKi, Moose, No Neck, and the rest of the casino fill Travis and Freddy with a desire to dig a deep hole and crawl into it.

Johnny Large basks in his public humiliation of Travis Best and Freddy Quigley, then whisks away with his too-thin and too-buff posse.

Perhaps if Johnny hadn't whispered into the muscle-bound ear of No Neck, the whole thing might have ended there.

Perhaps if Freddy's big brain hadn't noticed and instructed his feet to follow No Neck, that would have been that.

But no.

Travis follows Freddy, who quietly follows No Neck,

who walks to a private red phone, picks it up, and punches 444. He has no clue that four twelve-year-old eyes are glued to his every move.

Actually, No Neck is pretty much clueless about everything except how to make his body big, bigger, biggest, and how to hurt people bad, badder, baddest. No Neck feels lucky he has a job that so perfectly matches his muscular talents.

"Mr. Marshall, please, it's No Neck" he says in his steriod-choked No-Necky voice. "Yo, Bobby . . . Yeah, the usual . . . What are you, stupid? You gotta do it to them before they do it to you." No Neck grunts a muscle-bound laugh and hangs up.

The boys watch No Neck walk up to Cashier Window 7, grab a big bundle of chips, give one to the cashier, then walk them over to the diminutive Mr. Large, who does not thank him.

Freddy's brain buzzes and whirs. If he were a cartoon character, smoke would be shooting out of his ears and his hair catching on fire.

"Follow me," says Freddy.

Travis rolls his eyes, feeling disaster barreling toward them.

Still he follows.

A Hockey Puck, a Careless Pedestrian & a Circumcision

Blinding bright sunlight turns Travis and Freddy prickly-heated and squinty.

The casino-, restaurant-, and hotel-lined Strip buzzes like a hive full of high rollers, lowlifes, and middle-of-the-road fun lovers from the four corners of the round world.

A squadron of vibrant retirees shuffle by in shuffle-boardy shoes, deafening Bermuda shorts, and shrieking Hawaiian shirts, dark socks pulled up to knobby knees, with crowns of comb-overs and huge blue hair every-where, many wearing vast black sunglasses that seem to wrap all the way around their heads.

Freddy scans the aged crowd and zeroes in on Max and Maxine, who've been married fifty-five years, five months, and fifteen days.

"Excuse me," says Travis in his I'm-so-polite voice, "could you help us?"

"We're doing a little . . . uh," Freddy continues, "research, and . . ."

"Actually, we need someone to help us gamble," Travis finishes.

"A Rambler?" says Max in a too-loud voice. "Now that is a high-quality automobile. Yes, we had a Rambler in nineteen hunnert and fifty-six."

"No, we want you to place a bet," says Travis.

"A vet?" says Maxine. "Yes, Max is a vet, fought in the big one, WW II, the war to end all wars."

"Ee-wo Jee-ma," says Max.

"No thanks, we just ate," says Travis.

"What?" Max and Maxine say at exactly the same time.

"Thanks anyway," say Travis and Freddy at exactly the same time.

Travis and Freddy run into a short rotund man who is also old. His name is Don Rickles, and he likes to insult people by calling them hockey pucks.

Travis and Freddy have no idea that he is a very famous man.

"Excuse me, sir—" says Freddy.

Don Rickles cuts him off by saying:

"Why, did you pass gas?"

"What?" asks Travis.

"Huh?" asks Fred.

"What are you, a couple of junior hockey pucks?" rattles out of Don Rickles.

When the boys stare, pop-eyed and wide-mouthed,

Mr. Rickles sends this squirting out the side of his mouth:

"Hello? What are you, a milk shake short of a Happy Meal?"

"Uh—" says Freddy, trying to get them on track.

"We're looking for somebody to help us make a bet," says Travis.

"Don't look at me." Don Rickles shrugs so that his fat neck disappears. "I just lost five G's betting against myself, so gimme a break, huh?"

"No, really, this is a complete lock—" Travis insists.

"Oh, it's a lock, that's beautiful," Don Rickles barrels in. "From the mouths of babes. I love this town. Listen, I'd like to stay and chat, but I've got a circumcision I've got to get to—I'll save you a tip."

Don Rickles chuckles away as he saunters off.

"I'm hatin' this idea a lot." Travis shakes his head.

"The idea is good, it's the execution that's off," says Freddy. "Word of the day: *circumcision*."

"Go." Travis squints in intense concentration.

"'*Circumcision,* noun: a Jewish religious ceremony in which an infant has the tip of the male member cut off,'" says Freddy. "Now use it in a sentence."

"I would hate to have a circumcision today," says Travis.

"Me too," says Freddy.

Lady Luck now blows on Travis and Freddy's dice as a

cab screeches to a stop to avoid a careless pedestrian, and a cabby screams out the window.

Travis and Freddy swivel-head so they're staring at the angry cabby.

Sam.

"Saaaaaaaaaam!"

they yell as loud as they can.

Sam can't hear them, but as she starts to fishtail away, she feels a force following her, so instinctively she looks in her rearview mirror and sees two boys running toward her for all they're worth, screaming:

"Saaaaaaaaaam!"

A smile invades Sam's lips, and she hits the brakes, stopping her cab with another skidding squeal.

By the time the boys have sprinted to Sam's window, they're gasping Vegas air.

Sam, surprisingly happy to see them, says: "Hey, it's the Glimmer Twins outta Walla Walla. What's shakin', fellas?"

"Hey, Sam . . ." starts Travis, fighting for breath.

". . . a little help . . ." Freddy barks between breaths.

". . . tiny favor . . ." Travis manages to squeeze out.

"Is this some kind of charade thing?" Sam smiles like she hasn't smiled in a while.

"No, no, no," says Freddy.

"We need you to give us a hand. Trust us, Freddy's a genius," says Travis.

"You're a genius?" asks Sam.

"Yeah, he took a test, he's got a plaque from MIT and his own Web site and everything. You should check out his blog," says Travis, nodding his head proudly.

"Google QuigleyQool," finishes Freddy.

"And the point is . . ." says Sam.

"Uhhhh, it's complicated. But we wanna take you shopping," says Freddy.

"Shopping? What are we buying?" asks Sam, instantly interested.

"We're gonna get you a dress, and . . . whatever you need, plus we gotta buy some . . . stuff," says Freddy.

"What stuff?" asks Travis.

"Stink bombs, firecrackers, sparklers, you know, that kind of stuff," says Freddy.

"Okay . . . who's paying?" asks Sam, now keenly interested.

"We are," says Freddy.

"We *are*?" asks Travis.

"We are," says Freddy.

"You boys just said the magic word." Sam grins. *"Vamanos, muchachos."*

The boys jump into Sam's cab, oblivious to the disaster that awaits them thirty-five floors up as they hurtle through the traffic.

A Slinky Black Dress, a Lip Twitch & Happy Hands

"Heartbreak Hotel" pulses through the now meticulously clean Elvis Suite as another fabulous feast luxuriates on twin room-service carts.

Travis and Freddy are swallowed up in giant baby-bottom-soft bathrobes, watching Sam polish off a drumstick after she's wolfed her way through a whopping helping of spaghetti with meatballs.

Suddenly Sam stops, straightens up, and looks like she's trying to find something.

When she opens her mouth, a big brassy belch billows up her pipes and booms out of her mouth.

"Excellent tone." Travis nods.

"Outstanding resonance," agrees Freddy.

"Golf clap," says Travis.

Travis and Freddy golf-clap, fore and middle fingers tapping opposite palm in reverent appreciation.

"Thank you, thank you very much," Sam snarls like Elvis, complete with a quivering lip twitch.

Travis and Freddy laugh, even though they still have no idea who Elvis is.

"Why am I gettin' all dolled up?" Sam asks.

"Trust him, he's a—" Travis starts.

"I know, he's a genius, you told me that already." Sam smirks a chuckle. Then she gets serious and says, "But I'm tellin' ya right now, no funny stuff."

Travis and Freddy look hurt.

"We're from Walla Walla," Freddy explains. "We don't do funny stuff." Travis nods for emphasis.

"All right," says Sam, "but if you try any monkey business, I'm gonna smack you down. *Comprende?*"

"Yup," Travis and Freddy say with twin headshakes.

Sam dumps her beat-up leather bomber jacket and Yankees cap on the bed, grabs the two shopping bags, sashays into the bathroom, and locks the door behind her, while Travis and Freddy exchange a we-might-just-get-out-of-this-alive look.

"Okay, you ready to kick some blackjack butt?" asks Freddy.

"YEAHHHHH!"

Travis bellows. Freddy joins him, and together they yell:

"YEAHHHHH!"

Nine seconds later, Travis asks:

"How do you play blackjack again?"

Freddy rolls his eyes as he says:

"This is the last time I'm gonna explain this to you, so listen with your brain this time instead of your butt."

Travis nods through a laugh. "Good one."

"Thanks," Freddy says. "Okay, to win you gotta have a hand that adds up closer to 21 than the dealer. But if your cards add up to over 21, you lose. Busted. Jack, Queen, and King all count for 10, and an Ace can count as either 1 or 11. So, let's say you have a 6, a 7, and a 5." Freddy finds a 6, a 7, and a 5 from the deck and lays them out.

"And the dealer has an 8, an Ace, and a 10." Freddy lays down an 8, a 10, and an Ace.

"Who wins?"

Travis's head hurts as all the numbers mush together like potatoes mashing in his brain.

"Uhhhh, the uh, dealer . . . no me . . . no, the dealer . . . no, uh—" Travis stumbles and bumbles.

"6 plus 7 is 13. Plus 5 is 18, right?" Freddy tries not to sound like too much of a know-it-all, but does a very bad job of it.

"Whatever," says Travis.

"So you have 18, and the dealer has . . ." Freddy tries to wish the answer into the brain of Travis.

Travis's brain can't wrap itself around this unsolvable jumble of a puzzle.

This makes Freddy slap his palm onto the forehead protecting his big brain.

"19! 19!! 19!!! Remember what I said. An Ace is 11, or . . ." Freddy sounds like he's trying to lead a horse to water, and make it drink.

"I don't know." Travis sinks a little as his idiocy smacks him in his dull skull.

"1. An Ace is 11. Or 1." Freddy looks like he wants to shake some brains into his best friend's head.

But instead, he tries to reduce the thing to something so simple that even Travis will grasp it:

"You have 6 plus 7 plus 5. That's 18. The dealer has 8 plus 10 plus 1. That's 19. Who wins?"

"The dealer," Travis answers firmly. Even though he's sure he's right, he panics and begins to think maybe it was a trick question. So he asks: "Me?"

"No," says Freddy, resisting the impulse to call Travis

a troglodyte. "The dealer wins. He's closer to 21 than you, without going over."

"Oh, right," Travis says, almost understanding.

"Okay, here's how it works. First you put down whatever bet you want, you *ante up*. Then the dealer deals everybody two cards: one face down, and one face up. But both the cards he deals to himself are face up, so you can see them. Now everybody who wants to bet can bet again. If you want another card, you tell the dealer you wanna Hit. Then he gives you another card."

"Hit. Cool. Hit me." Travis imagines himself winning a bundle.

"Pay attention," says Freddy. "You can Hit as many times as you want. And every time before you Hit, you can bet again. If you don't wanna Hit, you Stick, and you get no more cards. The dealer has to take cards until they add up to 17. Once he gets to 17, he has to Stick, so he gets no more cards. If your first two cards add to 21, that's called Blackjack. Like, if you have an Ace and a King, for example." Freddy pulls an Ace and a King out of the deck.

If they could talk, the Ace and the King would say:

"Go back to Walla Walla. Now! Otherwise, Johnny Large will crush you like small pathetic bugs."

Unfortunately, these cards can't talk.

A woman in a slinky black dress, high-heeled spiky shoes, and black-banged wig, vavavavooms into the room.

Hard to believe, but the vavavavoomer is Sam.

"Bow wow wow!" barks Travis.

"Woof woof woof!" barks Freddy.

"Knock it off, ya knuckleheads! That ain't no way to treat a lady," Sam scolds.

"Sorry." They hang their heads together.

"Cool wig," says Freddy.

"You look better than Carolyn Strummeister," says Freddy.

"Seriously?" asks Sam.

"Oh yeah!" says Travis.

"Way better," says Freddy.

"Thanks," Sam says with a shocking (for her) amount of sweetness.

"Okay, let's play some blackjack," says Freddy.

"No way!" barks Sam. "I told you schmoes, no gambling."

"We're not," says Freddy.

"You are," says Travis.

"No way, absolutely not, forget about it." Sam's adamant.

"Sam, you just gotta trust us," says Freddy.

Sam busts up laughing.

"You don't know how many times I've heard that one."

"Just play some cards with us, that's all, and I'll show you how easy it is," says Freddy.

"No obligation, no risk." Travis sounds exactly like a TV spokesman as he trots out that million-dollar smile.

Sam studies the boys for a long time. She has a strong feeling in the pit of her peach that these two kooky kids are somehow, someway going to help in her relentless quest to save her dad. Usually, she ignores these feelings.

Not today.

So Sam sighs, nods her head, and says:

"All right. One hand."

Travis starts to deal, but when he does, it looks like he has seven thumbs.

Sam grabs the cards, smirks, then shuffles the deck six ways to Sunday: ruffling, cutting, making the cards dance in her hands, faster than the boys' eyes can see.

"CoooooooooooooooooooooooooooL!"

Travis and Freddy say through smiley faces.

"The ability to deal is what separates man from beast, you know," Sam says.

"Really?" Freddy says.

"For a genius, you're not too bright, are ya?" Sam smiles slyly and winks at Freddy.

Freddy shrugs. "I guess not."

"Okay, what are we playin'?" asks Sam.

"Blackjack," says Freddy.

Sam deals a King and a 7 to herself. Then a 10 and an unseen 6 to Travis. 16.

Travis looks to Freddy for advice.

Freddy gives him a you're-on-your-own-pal shrug.

"Uh, hit," says Travis, dripping with uncertainty.

Sam deals him a 9. Travis flips his unseen card. 25.

"Busted, boy," Sam teases good-naturedly.

Travis shrugs.

Freddy grins and gloats.

Sam deals five hands in a row.

Travis loses five hands in a row.

"Well," says Sam, "that was a very impressive display of how to lose A LOT of money in Vegas. Now, if you fellas don't mind, I've got places to go and people to see."

"Hold on," says Freddy, all excited. "We're not done yet." He turns to his best friend and says:

"Trav, if you'll do the honors."

Freddy hands Travis the extra-large, super-sparkly, crazy-pointy, cat-eyed old-lady glasses.

Travis slips them on.

"Nice look," Sam chortles.

"Why, thank you." Travis smiles, looking truly goofy.

Freddy retreats into the bedroom with his monster iBrain mega-laptop.

"Where's he goin'?" Sam asks.

Travis smiles like he knows a really great secret.

Through the glasses, Travis hears Freddy in his ear.

"Okay, champ, you're on."

Travis smiles his million-dollar smile at Sam and says:

"Freddy's going to powder his nose. Deal."

Sam rolls her eyes and deals.

Travis wins.

Sam deals another hand.

Travis wins.

Sam deals a dozen hands.

Travis wins them all.

Sam blows a low, I'm-impressed whistle and says:

"All right, how the hell did you do that?"

Freddy reappears from the bedroom, puts his iBrain on the table, then does a one-boy parade around the room, waving his hands over his head, conquering-hero style.

Travis makes crowd-going-crazy sounds.

"The Wonder Boy and the Gigabyte Kid, the pride and joy of Walla Walla, the underdogs, the dark horses, the kids from nowhere, are kicking some major butt in Vegas! And that's why they're such crowd favorites here in the Elvis Suite!"

Sam begins to smirk, but halfway through, the smirk blossoms into a chuckle and then a full-blown laugh.

I forgot how good it feels to laugh, Sam thinks as she says:

"Okay, spill it. How'd you do that?"

"It's a program I invented, based on multimodal basian probability theory and heterogeneous von Neumann network structure; once you get the prime numbers licked, the rest is elementary," says Freddy, like he's telling her that two plus two equals four.

"He talks like that all the time," says Travis. "I tried to tell you, but you wouldn't believe me."

"Okay," says Sam. "But how do you . . . I mean what are the glasses for?"

"Travis?" says Freddy.

"He can see what I see, he can hear what I hear, *and* he can talk to me," Travis says softly, like he's letting Sam in on a sweet secret.

Sam weighs the evidence carefully: magic granny glasses, iBraining kid genius, twelve wins out of twelve games.

Suddenly she smells money. Sees herself with a big pile of cash, hiring a fierce shark, which is a particularly vicious species of lawyer, to get her old man a retrial, celebrating a not-guilty verdict, watching him walk out of prison a free man at last.

Sam stares at Travis and Freddy. They look like such little kids. She sees herself busted, charged with corrupting minors, conspiracy, grand theft, and on and on.

"How old are you two anyway?" Sam asks.

"Thirteen," they say, proud as peacocks.

"Really?" Sam squints, skeptical.

"Almost." They nod together.

"Your parents know you're doing this?" she asks.

"Suuuuuuuuuuuuuuuuuuuuuure," Travis and Freddy assure, trying to look like they really mean it, but not fooling anyone.

Least of all Sam, who shakes her head, thinking:

Should I stay, or walk away?

A Long Minute, a Premonition & No Dorkage

When Sam strolls boldly into the nutty funhouse of the casino floor, decked out in all her vavavavoominess, topped off by the old-lady cat-eye glasses, she feels like a bizarro superhero: Groovin' Granny, half babe, half senior citizen, fighting crime and raking in the BIG MONEY.

A premonition is a feeling you get about something that's going to happen in the future. Sam now has one of these. Sam suspects, for some reason she can't quite figure out, that her life will never be the same.

She's right.

Back in the Elvis Suite, "Love Me Tender" plays as Freddy jacks his iBrain mega-laptop into the big TV. He and Travis stare at gamblers staring at Sam with an odd mix of delight and fright as the joint jumps, and suckers lose money as far as the eye can see.

"Sam, can you hear me?" Freddy asks into the microphone.

"Yup, you're coming in loud and—" Sam starts to say.

"Don't talk to us!" Travis and Freddy cut her off.

"Don't yell at me!" Sam barks.

A bouncer/Executioner gives her the hairy eyeball through the holes in his black hood.

"Just give a little nod for yes, or a little shake for no, you understand?" Freddy says.

Sam nods her head yes and smiles with as much innocence as she can muster at the bouncer/Executioner.

He smiles back and winks at her through an eyehole.

She does not wink back. Instead, she sees herself with her head on a chopping block about to be lopped off by the grinning idiot in the black hood.

"I did that, too, at first. I mean, talked out loud, it's hard not to," Travis says into the mike, trying to make Sam feel better.

Sam feels a little better.

"Okay, Sam, here we go," says Freddy. "Trav, you're on."

He picks up the phone that's wired into the iBrain, into which Freddy dials 444.

A voice answers.

"Mr. Marshall, please . . ." Travis makes his voice sound incredibly No Necky. It's weird to hear this stupid mooky muscleheaded voice coming out of Travis Best. "Yo, Bobby, it's No Neck . . . Yeah, the usual . . . Mr. Large is bankrollin' some babe. Hey, you gotta do it to them before they do it to you." Travis grunts a No Neck laugh. He hangs up, and then fist-pumps, and in his regular voice says:

"He shoots! He scooooores!"

"Okay, Sam, we're in," says Freddy into the mike. "Wait a minute, then go up to Window 7 and pick up the chips."

A minute is not very long.

Unless you're painfully waiting for it to pass, wondering if you're about to make the **BIGGEST** mistake of your life.

Then a minute is a very very long time.

"Whenever you're ready, Sam," says Freddy.

"Take a big breath," says Travis, trying to make Sam feel better.

Sam takes a big breath, and again she feels better.

"You're cool, Sam," says Freddy.

"Milky Way cool," says Travis.

As she gets to Cashier Window 7, Freddy says into the mike:

"Say, 'I'm here to pick up the chips from Johnny Large.'"

Sam is thrown by the mention of her dreaded enemy, the little man she's hated for so many years.

So this slips out of her mouth:

"I'm here to pick up the large from Mr. Chips."

Travis and Freddy exchange a horror-filled glance.

"What?" says Burt Mushnick, who's standing behind Window 7, looking stupefied in his stupid costume.

"Chips from Johnny Large, Sam!" Travis and Freddy say into the mike.

"Uh, sorry, yeah," says Sam. "Chips from Johnny Large, Sam."

"Who?" says Burt again.

"Don't say 'Sam,' Sam!" says Travis.

"What?" says Sam.

"What what?" says Burt.

"Just say, 'I'm here for the chips from Johnny Large,'" Freddy says slowly and carefully.

"I'm here for the chips from Johnny Large," Sam repeats slowly and carefully.

"Oh, Johnny Large, right." Burt's 'tude changes instantly from barely caring to barely hidden terror at the very mention of Johnny Large. "Why didn't you say so?"

This is the stupidest thing I've ever done, thinks Sam. And I've done some incredibly stupid things.

Burt slides $5,000 worth of chips toward her, along with a sick thin grin.

When Sam takes the chips and leaves, Burt's fake grin disappears.

"Phase One complete. Excellent work, Sam," says Freddy.

"And the crowd goes crazy," says Travis.

They make crowd-going-crazy sounds into the mike.

But as Sam leaves Window 7, she has a moment of clarity, where she sees exactly what she's doing.

Scamming Johnny Large.

"Big Mistake—" her brain screams.

Suddenly all her can-do gets up and goes, and she heaves a shaken sigh.

The boys hear it. Bad sign.

"Sam, it's okay." Freddy tries to sound calm.

"Really, it's okay, Sam." Travis does sound calm.

"Are you guys nuts?" says Sam too loud.

Everyone within twenty-feet radius stares at her like she's nuts.

She bolts with her chips.

"Where ya goin'?" Travis asks in partial panic.

"Sam, what's the matter?" Freddy asks in pure panic.

Sam walks quickly into the ladies' room, where women of all shapes, sizes, and colors are tucking in, painting on, and making delicate adjustments.

Shock flashes on the faces of Travis and Freddy as they yell:

"Hubba hubba, baby!
Wooooo wooooo!"

Sam slams into a stall, bangs the door closed, slaps the lock shut, whips off the glasses, turns them around, stares into them hard, and says:

"Knock it off!"

Sam's face fills the big TV in the Elvis Suite, where Travis and Freddy immediately shut up and look like they've been very bad boys.

"Don't Be Cruel" plays in the background.

"Have some respect, ya bozos. You wanna end up a couple of deadbeats?" Sam snarls on the big TV.

"No." Travis and Freddy lower their heads and mumble, "Sorry."

Sam plops on the toilet as she talks to the boys through the magic glasses:

"Look, I can't do this. You didn't tell me it was Johnny Large we were scammin'. Johnny Large? Are you kidding? I could get killed. Or worse, I could end up in jail, and then how am I gonna spring my old man?"

"Is she takin' a leak?" Travis whispers, confused.

"Beats me . . ." Freddy whispers back, confused.

"Sorry, boys, I just can't do it." Sam sighs. "No way."

"You got the chips, didn't you?" pleads Travis.

"Yeah," Sam has to admit as she puts the cat-eyed old-lady glasses back on.

"Just play a couple of hands, and if you don't like it, walk away," says Freddy, looking at the flat dull gray of the stall door on the big TV.

"No can do, boys." Sam flushes, rushes out of the stall, and slinks to a sink in front of a long mirror.

As she looks in the mirror, Travis and Freddy see Sam

in the old-lady glasses for the first time on their big TV.

She's the coolest dork ever.

When Sam looks down and turns off the faucet, Travis and Freddy see their lives going down the drain.

Sam looks in the mirror and mouths:

"Sorry."

Then she starts walking out of the bathroom, to give the chips back, return the old-lady glasses to the boys, and get on with the rest of her life.

And that would have been the end of the story. Except for the heartstopping urgency of Travis yelling:

"SAAAAAAAM STOOOOOPPPP!"

Sam stops.

"Sam, if you don't do this, I'm gonna lose my house, and my old man is gonna get hurt bad, maybe even killed," says Travis.

"Please, Sam—" Freddy pleads deeply.

"Pleeeeeeeeeeeeeeeeeeeeeeeeeeeeeease," Travis begs like he's never begged before.

Freddy's shocked that Travis, the too-cool-for-school kid, sounds like such a scared little boy.

Sam's touched by the anguish deep in Travis's voice. Suddenly she knows in her bones that this is her old man's Get Out of Jail Free card.

So she stares into the mirror and says:

"All right, I'll do it, but if you guys dork out on me,

I'm gonna personally see to it that you don't make it through puberty."

Sam's giant face on their titanic TV screen clearly means business.

"Zero dorking," assures Freddy.

"No dorkage," promises Travis.

With the boys' promise hanging in the air, Sam turns on her heels, squares her shoulders, and heads to the casino floor, where her fate awaits.

A Jack, a Blackjack & a Jackpot

excited yet terrified, Sam ambles through the electric atmosphere of the casino, trying desperately to be invisible. Every eye seems to spy on her. Every glance is a glare of terrible menace. Knees knocking, hands trembling, she wonders how her life has come to this.

Back in the Elvis Suite, Freddy kicks it into high gear.

"Trav, put a blank tape in the VCR and hit 'record,' will ya?"

"How come?" asks Travis.

"Look, if I can prove my probability theory works, I can get a free ride anywhere—MIT, Stanford, maybe even Reed College," explains Freddy, like he's telling Travis how water plus dirt equals mud. "And the tape will be proof."

"Whatever," says Travis, who plops in a blank tape and hits the red RECORD button.

Sam finds an empty blackjack table and sits.

Danny DiMollini, the dealer, dressed like a Knight, loves his job so much that he doesn't mind looking like an idiot in cheesy green tights, pointy shoes, and a chain-mail shirt.

The only thing he lacks is a wife.

But he's always looking.

Evaluating Sam as potential-wife material, Danny decides he likes the old-lady glasses and thinks she could be the one.

He smiles at her.

"Deep breath," Travis whispers into Sam's ear from the Elvis Suite.

Sam, about to face the first blackjack hand of the rest of her life, breathes deep.

She feels better.

On the giant screen in the Elvis Suite, superimposed over Danny DiMollini, the dealer, is a bunch of numbers, letters, boxes, and symbols. It looks like this:

		♥	♠	♦	♣
HIT	A				
	K				
STICK	Q				
	J				
BUST	10				
	9				
JACKPOT!	8				
	7				
	6				
	5				
$	4				
	3				
	2				

Freddy sits at the ready in front of his beloved iBrain.

"One hand, twenty bucks," he says.

Travis has that tingly, right-before-a-big-game feeling, butterflies the size of pterodactyls flapping around in his guts.

"Twenty?" asks Sam.

"Twenty?" asks Danny, loving the action.

"DON'T TALK TO US," Travis and Freddy repeat.

"All right, all right, keep yer pants on," says Sam without thinking.

She notices Danny looking at her like he can't decided whether she's fun or a freak. She knows that at any second he could push a button under the table that would make many cameras focus on her. And that can only lead to trouble of the Large variety.

"My pants?" Danny asks. You never know what kind of looney tune's gonna walk in here and make your day, Danny's thinking. Heck, she could be an award-winning ex–soap opera star. This, in fact, happened to him at this very table. A real nut job came in one night talking about all the millions she had. Turned out she wasn't really rich at all. She just thought she was 'cause her TV character was. She hardly spent any money, but she gave him a $500 tip. "You gotta love that," Danny says when he tells the story, which he does almost every day.

"Sorry," Sam replies in a deep voice she hopes makes

her sound like a reasonable human. "Just talking to my dear old dead mom."

Danny smiles back, thinking about his dear old living mom.

Sam puts a twenty-dollar chip on the table.

Danny the dealer deals. Sam puts her 9 and 3 right in front of the glasses so they show up giant on the TV in the Elvis Suite.

Freddy inputs the number 12 into his iBrain megalaptop.

HIT

Lights up on the TV screen, accompanied by the sound of a wood bat whacking a baseball.

"Hit," says Freddy like a scientist.

"Hit," says Travis like a kid who's a little too excited to be gambling.

Sam indicating she wants another card, says:

"Hit me."

Danny gives it to her: 7.

She holds up a corner of the card for Travis and Freddy to see.

Freddy inputs 19 into the iBrain.

STICK

Lights up, accompanied by the sound of a car screeching to a halt.

"Take another one." Freddy sounds like he knows exactly what he's doing.

"What?" Travis can't believe what Freddy is doing.

"What?" says Sam.

"What?" says Danny.

"Take a card," says Freddy.

"Why?" asks Travis.

"Nothing," says Sam to Danny.

"Okay," says Danny.

"We wanna lose this one," says Freddy.

"Ohhhhhhh," say Travis and Sam, understanding at exactly the same time, even though they're thirty-five floors apart.

"Don't talk to us!" Freddy says, like a scolding mom.

"Beg pardon?" says Danny.

"I think I'll take another card," says Sam.

"Certainly, ma'am," says Danny.

Danny gives her another card.

8.

Freddy inputs 27.

BUST

Lights up, with the sound of a loud wet fart splattering out of the big TV.

"Pardon me," say Travis and Freddy, bringing a smile to Sam's lips.

The $ box flashes:

–20

The TV groans.

"Oh darn, I lost," says Sam as Danny happily scoops up her cards and chip.

"Two hands. Fifty each," says Freddy flatly.

Sam puts down two fifty-dollar chips.

"Are we gonna win this time?" asks Travis.

"I certainly hope so," says Freddy.

"Cooool." Travis rubs his hands together.

Danny deals Sam two hands.

10 and 4.

2 and 7.

She lifts up the card corners for Travis and Freddy's viewing pleasure.

Danny deals a hand to himself.

10 and 8.

18.

Freddy inputs Sam's 14 and 9.

HIT

Flashes twice, followed by the sounds of two bats hitting two balls.

"Hit 'em both," says Freddy.

"Hit! Hit! Hit!" Travis bounces on the bed.

Sam nods to Danny that she wants two more cards.

The first card is revealed.

Queen of Spades.

"Whoops!" says Freddy, realizing he's made a mistake.

"Whoops?" Travis groans.

"Whoops?" Sam's distressed.

"Yeah. Whoops. I'm sorry. We lost. Do you guys mind?" Freddy snaps, annoyed.

"What happened?" asks Trav.

"It's early in the deck, it's just bad luck."

"Oh, great." Travis sulks. "That's just great."

Sam shakes her head, convinced that this was a BAD idea.

"Whoops?" Danny asks, more and more convinced that Sam is a famous nut job he can tell a colorful story about for many years to come.

BUST

Is followed a loud wet fart.

The $ box fills with this:

–70

The big TV groans.

"Yeah," says Sam, hoping to be adorable, "I goofed."

She's adorable, Danny thinks to himself.

Sam shivers a little as Danny deals her last card.

"Please, please, please, please, please," says Travis, like a kid who wants to win way too much.

Freddy wipes away the sweat globules accumulating on his face.

Jack of Diamonds.

19.

Travis, Freddy, and Sam win.

JACKPOT

Flashes on the screen, with the sounds of a cash register ringing, and a happy crowd going crazy.

The $ box says:

–20

Travis jumps up on Elvis's face, which grins from the bedspread, then bounces and down, yelling:

"JACKPOT!
JACKPOT!!
JACKPOT!!!"

Freddy does a little victory dance in his chair.

Sam tries not to smile, but fails.

"Congratulations." Danny smiles.

One of his favorite parts of the job is when people win money, especially if they're nice about it, which this wacky-glasses-wearing kook certainly is.

Sam smiles nicely. "Why, thank you."

"Okay, here we go." Freddy's all wired concentration. "Four hands, hundred on each."

"Are you nuts?" Sam spits.

"Yeah, baby, bring it on!" Travis trumpets.

"Beg pardon?" Danny's puzzled yet amused.

"I was . . . saying," says Sam, "'Do you have any nuts?' You know, Brazilian, macadamia, or just a regular old peanut."

"Of course." Danny motions to a waitress.

"Could you repeat that?" Sam says to Danny, even though she's actually talking to Freddy.

"I said, 'Of course,'" says Danny.

Then Freddy repeats, with authority:

"Four hands, a hundred on each."

"You sure?" asks Sam.

"No problem," says Danny, thinking what fun it is to be dealing to this whacked-out nut who just asked for nuts.

"Yes, four hands, hundred on each," Freddy repeats one more time with authority.

"And stop talking to us!" says Travis.

"You sure?" Travis whispers so Sam can't hear.

"Yes!" Freddy mouths, punctuated with a severe glare.

The nuts arrive via a waitress dressed as a Wench.

"Thank you." Sam smiles to the Wench/waitress, who smiles back.

She pops a cashew in her mouth and slides four hundred-dollar chips in front of her, causing Danny to deal Sam four hands.

Danny deals 18 to himself and says:

"The dealer has 18."

Sam studies the cards one after another as Freddy inputs.

The fourth hand is:

Jack of Diamonds and Ace of Spades.

BLACKJACK

Flashes on the screen, with the sounds of fireworks, crazy crowd, and bells ringing their heads off.

"We're goin' to CyberWorld, baby!" Travis dances around the Elvis Suite.

Freddy looks peeved as he turns to Travis and says:

"Do you mind? I'm tryin' to work here."

Travis whispers:

"Sorry."

Freddy makes the necessary calculations, the screen hits and sticks, whacks and screeches, until all four hands are played out.

Sam exposes her cards, one by one.

19, 20, 19, and 21.

Sam tries hard to look humble. It's not easy.

The gathering crowd buzzes.

Danny's overjoyed. He sees a human-interest story in the newspaper about him, this semifamous wacko, and her wacky winning streak.

The $ box goes to:

$380

"Who's your mommy, who's your daddy, who's yer little bitty bay-beee!" Travis chants.

Danny happily hands Sam her winnings.

"Why, thank you," she says.

"You're welcome," says Danny, who is loving all of Sam's politeness.

Freddy says:

"Okay, Sam, here we go: four hands, thousand on each."

"Oh yeah, baaa-by!" Travis says as he struts around the room like he's leading a marching band.

"Huh?" Sam says with disbelief.

"What?" asks Danny again.

"Four hands, thousand bucks on each." Travis leans into the mike, trembling with adrenaline.

"I, uh . . . I love your nuts," says Sam, who then eats a macadamia nut.

She puts down four thousand-dollar chips.

Danny smiles, dealing out four hands, bubbling with fun, feeling a hot streak coming on, the crowd oohing and aahing.

Sam shows Freddy the cards. He inputs. Lights flash and sounds pour roaring from the TV.

"Hit on one and three, Stick on two and four," Freddy says with utter confidence.

Sam motions to two of her hands.

Danny deals.

Chips are slid.

Sam slowly turns over her cards.

She wins three more hands, and when all the bells and whistles stop ringing and blowing, the tote board reads:

$3,380

"Freddy, you're a monster, you're a killer, you're my hero, man!" Travis has never even come close to admitting this to Freddy, even though secretly it's always been true.

"Thank you, I cannot deny it, I am the greatest!" Freddy mock bows.

Both believe that this is confirmation of the inevitable greatness their simultaneous births hint at.

They do their fist-bump-chest-bump-snap-fingers-to-six-shooter ritual.

In the background, they hear Danny saying happily: "Congratulations again."

Sam looks down, and the boys see their winning chips sliding toward them.

"Thank you ever so much," Sam says with all the modesty she can muster. "Must be my lucky day."

More people gather around the edges of the table, drawn like moths to the flame of BIG BIG MONEY.

In the Elvis Suite, "(I'm Just a Hunka Hunka) Burning Love" wails as Travis sweats bullets, higher than a kite, and Freddy just keeps busting moves.

Hand after hand, hand over fist, they win and win again and again, raking in the chips, losing few and far between.

As some dust settles, the $ box reads:

$68,500

"Okay," says Freddy, getting tougher and more focused by the second. "Five hands, five thousand on each."

Travis sucks in his breath and says:

"Five G's, holy moley!"

He hopes it never ends. Travis is definitely his father's son.

Sam is sipping cold mineral water when she hears Freddy tell her to bet twenty-five G's.

She accidentally spits water out of her mouth. Sometimes comedians do this on purpose. It's called a spit take. It's hard not to be funny doing a spit take.

Thirty-five floors above, Travis and Freddy can't stop laughing.

Danny ducks just in time to miss Sam's spritz, then laughs. He can't wait to tell his mom about this kooky chick.

"You okay?" Danny asks Sam.

At the same instant the boys say:

"You okay?"

"Yeah, sorry." Sam wipes everything down with a napkin. "Just went down the wrong pipe."

"A kick save and a beauty, by Sam, the Queen of Cool," crows Travis.

"Smooth move, Ex-Lax," says Freddy into the mike with a chuckle and a smirk.

Sam lays out five piles of $5,000 chips. Low whistles wind-chime from the crowd with some woo-hooing and a few "oh yeahs."

Danny smiles and deals her five more hands.

At this exact instant, in the Security Room, where monitors display every square inch of the Excalibur Hotel & Casino, Tony Baretta, an ambitious young man who dreams of one day owning his own hotel/casino, just happens to reach for his coffee and, finding his cup empty, gets so angry that he punches himself in the leg, causing him to look around the room to see if anyone observed him having an anger-management problem. This causes him to see Sam on a screen placing five $5,000 bets as the crowd hummingbirds around her. Something about the strange combination of vavavavoom, old-lady cat-eye glasses, and twenty-five grand makes his nose twitch.

Trouble.

He switches the camera trained on Sam and Danny to his monitor and watches very closely. He's got a feeling about her. Hinky. That's what he thinks she is.

Sam picks her cards up and flashes them to Freddy, who inputs furiously.

Danny has a 7 and a 10.

17.

"The Gigabyte Kid is hard at work, folks, his eyes are on fire, and the crowd is going KA-razy." Travis makes a crowd-going-crazy sound while the crowd around Sam throbs.

"Tell her to stall a second," says Freddy.

"Stall a second," says Travis into the mike.

"How?" says Sam.

"What?" says Danny.

"What?" says Sam.

"Talk about your mother," says Travis.

"Beg your pardon?" Danny's excited to see what's coming next.

"I was just thinking about my dear old mom," Sam says.

"Really?" Danny starts thinking about his own mother, wondering whether she'd like this kook in the funny cat-eye glasses.

"Hurry up, Freddy," says Travis, his heart pumping like Speed Racer.

"She was a glorious woman," says Sam, who, like Freddy, never knew her mother. "A saint, really."

"That's so nice," says Danny, who likes a person who loves her mother.

"And when I find myself in times of trouble, she comes to me," says Sam.

Finally, the computer flashes the results.

"Hit on one, Stick on two and three, and Hit on four and five," says Freddy.

Sam, relieved, indicates to Danny where she's hitting and sticking.

Danny deals, very much enjoying this new twist of the talking dead mother.

Everything gets extra quiet now as everyone waits for her to reveal her hands.

Travis drops to his knees and starts praying.

"Please, oh please, oh please, if we win, I'll never do anything bad ever again."

Suddenly the bigness of it hits Freddy, and he puts his head between his hands.

Tony Baretta eagle-eyes Sam's every move.

Danny looks at his 17.

Sam, pretending to act extra casual, turns over her hidden cards:

20, 19, 21, 19, 20.

ALL WINNERS!

Freddy inputs the result. The computer screams:

JACKPOT!
JACKPOT!
JACKPOT!

Travis is the first to go berserk, rolling around like a cat full of nip, then howling like a dog at the moon.

"AHHHHHHHH-

OOOOOOOOOO!"

Freddy jumps out of his chair and starts screaming:

"The rookies outta Walla Walla, Washington, are conquering Lost Wages, and the crowd goes crazy!"

Travis makes his crowd-going-crazy sound even as the crowd around Sam goes crazy.

They both sound like this:

"Ahhhhhhhhhhhhh!!!"

Travis starts chanting:

"Fredddy!!!
"Fredddy!!!
"Fredddy!!!"

Danny can't believe her luck as he hands Sam her winnings. He doesn't know that luck has nothing to do with it.

Sam adds her new chips to the already-large stack sitting in front of her like mini–money pancakes as people she's never met pat her on the back, try to buy her drinks, and tell her how great she is.

She's the star of the show, and she loves it.

"America's an amazing country, am I right, folks?" Sam asks the crowd.

They roar approval.

Meanwhile, Tony Baretta, suspecting the foulest of play, is calling Mr. T, the next guy up the Excalibur food chain.

Travis throws his arms around Freddy and puts his forehead on his best friend's. Then they shake and scream like never before:

"YEAAAAAAAAH!"

Travis can practically see the look of relief on his parents' faces when they realize he's solved all their problems.

This causes Freddy to see it, too.

The $ box flashes:

$250,130

In the afterglow, Freddy leans into the mike and says:
"Okay Sam, that's it, cash in, we're done."

"What?" asks Sam in disbelief.

"What?" asks Danny with a smile.

"What?" asks Travis in disgust.

"I told you," says Freddy, "we get to two-hundred-fifty, we quit."

"Are you crazy? We're on a roll. This thing's a solid lock," Travis rages.

"No," says Freddy coolly, "we agreed. At two-hundred-fifty, we quit."

"You're really pissing me off," says Trav.

"Bite me," says Freddy. "Sam, cash in and walk away."

"I said, 'I hope this never ends, and why should it?'" Sam says this so Freddy knows she's really talking to him.

"Absolutely," agrees Danny, who mistakenly thinks she's talking to him.

"I hear my old mother tellin' me to quit, but you don't want me to do that, do you, folks?" Sam turns to the crowd.

"*No!*"

"*No way!*"

"Heck no!"

The crowd, having tasted blood, wants more.

Meanwhile, thirty-five floors above, Travis turns red as he sees red, then turns to Freddy and says:

"What are you, stupid?"

"I'm telling both of you, that's it, we're done, finito, get outta there, Sam." Freddy's firmer than he's ever been.

"We can go all night, man, it's a LOCK!" Travis's eyes have gone wild.

"Well, it seems like dear old mom's a bit of a stick-in-the-mud, and she wants to just fold up the tent," says Sam.

The crowd moans:

"Noooooooooooooo!"

Danny doesn't say anything, but he doesn't want her to quit either.

"You guys are making me sick," Freddy says with disgust. "If we don't quit now, someone's gonna catch on, and then we'll be in SERIOUS trouble."

He doesn't know, of course, that they're already in SERIOUS, SERIOUS, SERIOUS trouble!

"Don't punk out on me, Freddy," snarls Travis. "Time to stand up and be a man."

Sam takes off the old-lady glasses and looks into them as she pretends to wipe the lenses with a bar napkin. Knowing full well she's filling the big screen in the Elvis Suite, she says:

"I ain't stoppin' now, Mama!"

And with that the crowd lets out a whoop:

"WHOOOOOOOOOOOOP!"

As she puts the glasses back on, Freddy says in a voice that's never come out of him before, one that sounds like it knows exactly what it's talking about:

"It's over, Sam. Walk away, now!"

It stops Sam cold, like a wake-up call when you're late on your first morning at a new school.

Sam suddenly sees herself stealing from Johnny Large, cheating the casino, losing her head in the excitement of the winning, and making herself the center of all this attention when she's supposed to be blending in so nobody notices her.

Danny immediately senses the change in Sam. He knows it's over. It's sad, but it was fun while it lasted, he muses.

Sam says loudly so Freddy can hear:

"I hear ya, Ma, time to pack it up."

The crowd groans as Sam gets up to leave.

"Thanks for the memories," says Sam, handing Danny a thousand-dollar chip.

"Why, thank you." Danny takes the chip and waits with glee for Sam to reveal what famous crackpot she is.

Imagine his surprise when she assembles her chips, nods to the crowd, walks over to a cashier window, and cashes them without a word.

$249,130.

"(Let Me Be Your) Teddy Bear" plays in the Elvis Suite as Travis loses it:

"Why don't you go change your diapers, you little pantywaist. I'm always stickin' up fer you, I'm always saying, 'No, Freddy's cool, Freddy's all right.' But you know what, everybody's right, you *are* a loser."

"Shut up, Travis." Freddy's trying not to take it personally as his best friend slashes away at his soft underbelly.

Travis fills with so much raging adrenaline that he shoves Freddy backward into the wall, screaming:

"What's wrong with you, ya little punk! This is a solid LOCK. See, this is why nobody at school likes you. Nobody likes you, man. Nobody. 'Cuz you're weak, and you're a geek, and you're a freak. And from now on, I'm not hangin' out with you anymore. Just forget we ever met, 'cuz you are a loser, and you'll always be a loser."

Travis goes to push Freddy again, but this time Freddy doesn't let him. This time Freddy fights back.

Travis, his face furious red, turns his hands into fists of fury. He cocks one and is just about to punch Freddy in his long nose.

"Go ahead, hit me!" Freddy screams. "Punch me in the face. Is that what you wanna do?"

Travis looks down at his clenched white fist.

"This isn't some game, Trav." Freddy's voice is suddenly lower than it's ever been. "This is serious. Look at yourself, man. You wanna end up like your dad?"

Travis stops. Sees his father, broken, losing the house, going to jail, his mom's too-sad face. He looks in the mirror. His face turns into his father's. His fist turns back into a hand as he sinks onto the bed. He feels the tears starting to spill over the dam. He barely stops them.

A cold front of sad moves in, and a chill fills the room.

Freddy walks over to the bed, sits down next to his best friend, and says:

"Trav, I'm sorry, I was just tryin' to . . ."

"No man, *I'm* sorry, you're right . . ." Travis says.

Try as he might, Travis can't hold back the tears anymore. They fill up his eyes, and when his eyes get too full, they fall down his face.

"Trav," Freddy says soft, "I'm really sorry . . . about your dad and all . . ."

"Yeah," Travis almost says.

"Ya gotta promise me one thing," says Freddy.

"What?" Travis says.

"You're never gonna do this again," says Freddy.

"Never, man. Never again."

The tears now stop.

They sit in a new silence.

They sit this way for a long time.

Nobody knows what to say.

Suddenly something dawns on Freddy, and he says into an imaginary mike:

"Travis Best, you just beat the house in Vegas, you just saved your house in Walla Walla, what are you gonna do now?"

He thrusts the fake mike in front of Travis, who leans into it and says:

"I'm goin' to CYYYYYYBERRRRRWOOOOOOO-OOORLD!"

Thirty-five floors below, Sam walks away from the teller, high as a kite, with $249,130 in her purse.

Tony Baretta calls Burt Mushnick at the teller window.

"Did you give a buncha chips to some dame in strange old-lady glasses earlier?"

"Sure, I remember her, boss," Burt says, all flustery. "She got five thousand in chips from Johnny Large. No Neck authorized it."

Tony Baretta hangs up. He can feel fishiness deep down in his gills.

He calls No Neck.

"Did you authorize some broad to draw five G's for Johnny Large?"

"No," says No Neck, annoyed to be torn from his power lifting.

"You sure?" asks Tony Baretta.

"Yeah," No Neck snaps, flat as the hair atop a Marine's head.

Tony Baretta feels No Neck's steroid-fueled rage ripping through the phone and right into his head. It takes a great deal of effort to calmly say:

"Okay, thanks."

No Neck hangs up the phone like he wants to crush it into dust.

Tony Baretta hangs up, glad, and grins, thinking that maybe he can get on the good side of the little gangster man.

Travis and Freddy bounce up and down on the head of Elvis, which is printed on the bedspread, while screaming:

"CYYYYYBERWOOOOOOOOO-OOORLD!"

Peaceful Geese, 85 One-Armed Bandits & Misery's Company

lue Suede Shoes" plays as Sam sashays full of attitude and money into the Elvis Suite and plants kisses on Travis, then Freddy. The boys blush, although neither of them will admit it later.

Freddy heads where he always heads when he's embarrassed: his beloved iBrain mega-laptop.

He punches in some numbers, then says:

"I got us booked on the next flight home; we leave in about three hours."

"Okay, but first," says Sam, "I'm taking you two goons out to celebrate!"

"Cooooooooooool," Travis and Freddy coo.

As Freddy starts packing, Travis begins fiddling with Freddy's iBrain, looking for a video game Freddy invented called *Smash the Heads of People You Hate*.

This makes Freddy whip his head around sharp and snap:

"Don't touch that, ya streptococcus."

"Shut up, fungi!" says Travis.

"Fungi is plural, I would be a fung-*us*," says Freddy.

"Whatever," says Travis.

"Word of the day," says Freddy. "*Peptic ulcer:* noun, a break in skin or mucous membrane characterized by loss of surface tissue, disintegration, and often pus, caused by the stomach producing excess pepsinic acid."

"Cool." Travis nods, taking it all in. After he thinks a moment, he says, "I can't eat any more of this cake, my peptic ulcer is starting to drip pus."

"Excellent." Freddy laughs.

As Sam watches the boys, she finds herself thinking: I wish I had a best friend.

Suddenly all hell breaks loose inside Freddy's iBrain mega-laptop; it whirs and grinds, and the big TV fills with gobbledygook.

Travis looks mortified.

Freddy grabs his trusty iBrain, which has been better to him than any human being, while fuming at Travis.

"Travis, you are a serious knuckleheaded lug. It really is like you have knuckles in yer head."

As Freddy punches some buttons and manipulates his mouse, Travis says:

"Sorry, man."

After much high-level fancy-pants digital trickera-tion, Freddy calms down his iBrain.

But suddenly the master plan for the Excalibur

appears on the big TV: electrical system, security, air-conditioning ducts, heating system, personnel records, one-armed-bandit computers, roulette-wheel controls, and on and on and on.

"I don't know how you did it, but we hacked in, baby," says Freddy, his big brain shifting into fifth gear. "Watch this."

The main floor of the casino appears on the TV.

Freddy hits a couple of buttons, then pushes:

RETURN

Eighty-five one-armed bandits hit three cherries all at the same time, coins flowing from every one of those machines like golden lava. Eighty-four customers scream with glee. The eighty-fifth customer, Doris Delveccio, from Owl's Head, Maine, believes this is a miracle of God and passes out.

Pandemonium grips the casino floor, money shoved into bulging pockets, grizzled veterans with mouths agape, security going ballistic trying to keep it calm. No one has ever seen this much coin fall out this many machines all at the same time.

Travis, Freddy, and Sam crack up.

"Jackpot!"

Freddy keeps hitting buttons on his iBrain, and different rooms flash by.

Johnny Large appears, sitting in his suite. Which just happens to also be on the thirty-fifth floor.

"Hey, it's Johnny Large," says Freddy.

On the big screen, the little Mr. Large sits next to No Neck, who's doing curls with weights the size of a Shetland pony.

Across from them sits Dan Kong, a man with hair bolting straight up out of his head, standing there like it's been scared straight.

"And who's that guy?" asks Travis.

"Whatta you got, ragwort for brains?" says Freddy. "That's Dan Kong—"

"Noted fight promoter and scumbucket," says Sam.

Johnny Large opens a briefcase full of money and hands it to Dan Kong.

Kong smells the money like it's sweet perfume, then shakes hands with Johnny Large and says:

"On behalf of my most exalterated client, it is my delectation to expresserate our gratitudation, and pronouncicate with absolutitude that the bout will have extreme exterminatiousness in round number five, and that's no jive."

"Excellent," says Johnny Large.

Dan Kong closes the briefcase and smiles a smile that wants to be a million dollars, but stops at about a buck fifty.

Then Kong is gone.

Travis and Freddy shake their disbelieving heads.

Sam nods hers knowingly.

"Did what I think just happened happen?" Travis asks.

"Did Large and Kong just fix this weekend's fight?" asks Freddy.

"Sure smells that way," says Sam.

"Shouldn't we tell somebody?" asks Freddy.

"Who you gonna tell?" challenges Sam.

"The cops—" says Travis.

"The feds—" says Freddy.

"Yeah, right, what are you gonna say?" Sam smirks. "That after you scammed five grand outta Johnny Large, then ripped off the casino for two-hundred-and-fifty G's, then tapped into their security cameras, you saw Mr. Vegas rig the heavyweight championship? Are you gonna tell 'em this before or after you tell 'em you're twelve years old?"

"Thirteen," say Travis and Freddy.

Sam stares at them, hands on her hips.

"In a week," Travis and Freddy admit weakly.

After a moment, Freddy nods.

"I see your point."

"So what do we do?" asks Travis.

"Get outta Dodge," says Sam.

"You mean Vegas?" asks Freddy.

"Bingo," says Sam.

Suddenly she stops. Imagines herself hiring a hotshot

lawyer and getting her dad released from the pokey. She shakes her head in amazement. Can't believe they actually got away with it. When Sam looks at Travis and Freddy, a wave of appreciation washes over her, and she's overwhelmed by the desire to thank them in a way they will truly appreciate.

Suddenly she shoots the boys a sly smile and says:

"Let's adios."

"Where?" ask Travis and Freddy.

"All You Can Eat!" says Sam.

"ALL YOU CAN EAT!" the boys shout.

Sam grabs the Boy Scout satchel where the cash is stashed and says:

"Always keep the cash on hand. Remember, cash is king."

Travis and Freddy nod in confusion.

"I thought Elvis was king," says Freddy.

Sam laughs.

"You two are a panic."

As they leave the Elvis Suite with the satchel-toting Sam, "Blue Christmas" starts to play.

At that exact second, the phone rings in the suite of Johnny Large. This annoys No Neck, because he has to stop doing his curls just as he's getting to the burn.

"Yeah, just a minute," No Neck grunts into the phone.

"Gimme that," says Johnny Large.

No Neck hands him the phone, and after listening hard, Large barks:

"What?"

After he listens for twenty-two more seconds, he says through a bugged-out face:

"Let me understand this: Some broad in goofy glasses schlemieled two hundred and fifty G's outta the casino, bankrolled by *my* five Gs?"

His blood pressure spikes, his breath gets short, and his brainpan fries.

Johnny's nasty old man died of high blood pressure when he was fifty-two.

Johnny Large just turned fifty-two. He believes he's going to go the same way. Any day now.

When he feels his blood pressure rise, Johnny Large has been advised to picture a happy place. So he now pictures a lake with a cabin he used to get taken to when he was eight, before his mean dad died of high blood pressure.

In the tiny skull of Johnny Large, he sees peaceful geese flying in formation over the pond.

This calms Large.

"Stop," he says quiet into the phone. "Who *is* this dame?"

Large listens, then spits:

"I am confused and bamboozled, and also I do not understand what you are allegedly talking about. Stop now before I send a large man to deposit you on your head. Tell me this: *Where* is she? . . . The Elvis Suite? Thank you. You're fired. Good-bye."

The diminutive Johnny Large smashes the phone down, turns to the huge Moose and the equally large No Neck, then says:

"Why are you two mooks still present, and also here?"

"Uh . . ." Moose is all stupid.

No Neck says nothing. He knows it's a trick question, that no matter how he answers, it'll be wrong, and Johnny Large'll rip him up one side, then down the other, front and back. Either way, he'll still have to go and find the broad in the funny glasses, so he decides it's better to keep his yap shut.

"Don't say 'uh', ya mook. Go and find this broad who is taking my cabbages, and bring her to me, with the cabbages of the casino, along with my personal cabbages."

Johnny Large waves them away with his child-size hand.

The twin muscles clump out.

Johnny Large yells:

"KiKiKi!"

No one answers.

KiKiKi the supermodel left thirty-four minutes ago.

Without even saying good-bye.

The minuscule Johnny Large now vows to make the broad in the glasses, and whoever she's in with, suffer the way he now suffers.

Misery, you see, loves company.

16

A Pig Nose, Jimmies & Pongo Faaoulaafaafuulaa

Sam, Travis, and Freddy wade elbow-deep into mounds of mashed potatoes awash with waves of gravy; a bevy of burgers, snow-capped milk-shake mountains, gigantic jiggling Jell-O heavy with suspended fruit, a feast of roast beast, and a cornucopia of corn dogs, cookies, and cakes cover the table.

They are surrounded by people of all races, creeds, colors, and supersizes grazing, gulping, and gorging at the Swine and Bucket All You Can Eat buffet.

"Glorp shtrumpl klwrt," says Travis.

"Blort truswrt wekldrnf," replies Freddy.

"Nluutr digglergh twndf," adds Sam.

They have no idea that even as they eat all they can eat, the gooney Moose and the menacing No Neck are showing pictures of Sam (one with old-lady glasses, one without) to BB Rebowski, the Excalibur doorman, who is dressed like Shakespeare.

"I don't know," says BB.

BB really does know, but he wants to get money for

the information. He believes this is the American way, that this is why his parents escaped the Olde Country to come to the land of milk and money. BB just wants his milk and his money.

"Look," says No Neck, appearing bored and deadly at the same time, "this is for Johnny Large."

"Oh, why didn't you say so?" says BB. Much like his Olde Country ancestors, he feels a deep sense of loyalty, respect, and awe for the King, in this case the Napoleonic Johnny Large. To do a service for the King is a duty, an honor, and a privilege. "For Johnny Large, I would do anything. Yeah, she went with some kids down to the Swine and Bucket."

"Kids?" asks Moose.

"Kids," says BB.

"Thanks," says No Neck, as he expertly palms BB a hundred dollars.

America, what a country! BB thinks as he watches the muscle waddle away.

No Neck and Moose stomp off into the neoned Vegas dusk, clomp into the Swine and Bucket, and scope the chirping, slurping, burping masses.

They confront the maître d', Peter Paul Provologna, who is wearing a pig nose and pig ears. They ask if he's seen Sam. He also pretends not to know, because he too wants money for the information.

Unfortunately for him, No Neck is grumpy because

his swollen body is packed with too many steroids, so he picks Provologna up by the throat, slams him back into a wall, and holds him there.

Provologna gasps for air, fears for his life, and points at Sam.

Jackpot!

As Sam, Travis, and Freddy respectively suck down Jell-O, potato, and roast beast, No Neck drops Provologna, who plops on the floor.

Remarkably, his pig nose and pig ears remain perfectly in place.

No Neck and Moose, five hundred pounds of twitching meat, now hover over Sam and our heroes, who look up with stuffed mouths.

Travis and Freddy, terrified and trying not to show it, look to Sam. She gives them a calming it's-all-good wink, then says:

"Sorry, fellas, the Big and Stupid Convention is next door."

Travis and Freddy nod in appreciation and give Sam a golf clap.

"Johnny Large requests to see you," says No Neck.

"I'll handle this," says Travis. "Actually, our schedule is kinda jammed right now, but if he wants to make an appointment, we can maybe fit him in next week."

"You don't understand, this is not a request—" Moose starts, but Freddy cuts him off.

"But he just said it *was* a request," says Freddy. "'Johnny Large *requests* to see you,' that's what you said."

"Kid's gotta point," adds Sam. "Seriously, we're doin' an All You Can Eat thing here, and we got a lotta eatin' left to do," adds Sam.

"All You Can Eat," Travis and Freddy repeat.

"Maybe you didn't understand. Johnny Large needs to see you—" starts Moose.

"Now!" finishes No Neck.

"Why don't you guys join us—you look hungry. The mashed potatoes are excellent, aren't they, boys?" says Sam.

"They're refulgent," says Travis.

"They're munificent," says Freddy.

Sam flings a massive spoonful of mashed potato and gravy at No Neck, hitting him right in the left eye.

Diners stop and stare. When they laugh, Moose has a hard time not laughing, too.

No Neck, blinded in one eye, freaks, flailing his huge brutish side-of-beef arms, backing into the five-foot six-inch, 314-pound Pongo Faaoulaafaafuulaa, a Samoan, who is currently carting 7.8 pounds of food back to his table.

Everyone stops laughing.

Pongo Faaoulaafaafuulaa, instinctively believing he's being attacked, drops his tray and begins wrestling furiously with the mashed-potato-blinded No Neck.

Diners gape at what looks like two prehistoric mutants grappling for grub.

As chaos reigns, Travis and Freddy launch handfuls of banana split at the steroid-bloated head of Moose looming over them. Ice cream, whipped cream, nuts, cherries, congealed hot fudge, and jimmies splatter all over it.

"Split!" yells Sam.

Moose frantically tries to wipe goo from his eyes as No Neck is locked in mortal combat with Pongo Faaoulaafaafuulaa, who just came here to eat all he could.

Sam, Travis, and Freddy slip through the mess and bolt out the back door, moneybag in hand.

Moose, on the other hand, slips *in* the mess, and falls in a heap of glop.

Fourteen minutes later, bent over in an alley behind something that looks remarkably like an Egyptian pyramid, Sam, Travis, and Freddy have run out of breath, and they're trying to get some of it back.

"You think we lost 'em?" pants Travis.

"I think we lost 'em," pants Freddy.

"Yeah, I think we lost 'em," pants Sam.

They breathe easy, turn a corner, and head for Sam's cab.

Instead they slam straight into knuckleheaded No Neck and menacing Moose, bruised, gooed, and aching to hurt our heroes.

"Hey, Gorgeous, you and your boyfriend ain't lookin' so good." Sam smirks a chuckle.

Travis and Freddy whip out smirky chuckles of their own.

When No Neck picks up Travis in his left hand and Freddy in his right hand, the boys lose their smirks and their chuckles.

But even though she's FREAKING OUT, when Moose hoists Sam up, she never loses hers.

Goofy Peepers, Dangling Monkey Boys & Hard Knocks

travis and Freddy quiver in the gargantuan suite of the midget-size Johnny Large, trying to look innocent, knowing they're guilty as sin on a stick.

Sam, tied to a chair and desperately wanting to remain in disguise, still wears the old-lady cat-eye glasses, claiming she can't see a thing without them.

Johnny Large, pound for pound the meanest human on the planet, is beside himself as he paces his monster luxury suite, irate that he can't for the life of him figure out how he knows Sam.

"Seriously, from where do I know you from?" he asks her for the seventeenth time.

"I opened for Wayne Newton last night," Sam cracks wise. "Maybe you caught the show."

The boys laugh. Bad move.

"SHUTTUP!" screams Johnny Large.

Silence.

Travis and Freddy wear twin masks of mute terror.

Sam tries her smirk-and-chuckle, but neither is working at the moment.

"Seriously, from where do I know this broad from?" Johnny Large asks No Neck and Moose, who have changed into clean tight-fitting shiny suits.

They do tiny twin thick-neck shrugs.

"Remove the glasses," says Johnny Large.

No Neck removes them.

Sam glares.

"Unremove the glasses," says Johnny Large.

Glasses back on.

Johnny Large shakes his little head.

He just hates when he can't place a face.

"Somebody better tell me from where I know this broad from!!!" Johnny Large bellows.

No one says nothing.

Johnny Large, trying hard to stop his skyrocketing blood pressure, visualizes the geese flying by his pond, breathes easier, then chuckles.

"Some broad in goofy peepers and two little monkey boys. You really thought you were gonna jackroll *Johnny Large*? That is humorous, amusing, and also funny."

Nobody laughs.

"Are you not amused?" asks Johnny Large.

Suddenly No Neck and Moose realize they're supposed to laugh.

So they laugh. But the laughs ring hollow and fake and make everything seem worse instead of better.

"Did you *really* think you were gonna hoist five G's offa *Johnny Large*?" asks the tiny yet incredulous Johnny Large.

"Uh, yeah," says Travis.

Freddy does not realize this is a trick question and that any answer will be wrong. So he says:

"Actually, a hoist is a mechanical device used to lift something, it's like a winch. I think you meant *scam*. And technically, yes, we *did* scam five grand from you."

Sam rolls her eyes.

"NOBODY makes a monkey outta Johnny Large! NOBODY!" screams the diminutive Johnny Large.

Travis and Freddy pull back, trembling.

"WHO makes a monkey outta Johnny Large?" roars the minute Johnny Large.

"Nobody." Travis and Freddy shake, scared spitless.

"And who are you little MONKEY BOYS?"

"Nobody," Travis and Freddy whisper, whimpering witlessly.

Geese on the pond, geese on the pond, geese on the pond, Johnny Large says to himself, trying to keep his little head from exploding off his wee body.

"Disrobe yer clothes," he says to the boys, very flat, as if he were saying: "I think it's gonna rain tomorrow."

Our heroes don't understand. They look at Sam, who

gives a whattayagonnado? shrug, then says to Johnny Large:

"Look, they had nothin' to do with any of this, whatever it is, so let 'em go, they're just little kids."

Travis and Freddy put on their best little-kid faces and shrink a little more.

"Disrobe yer clothes," Johnny Large says, much harder this time.

This time the boys are so confused they don't do anything, except ask:

"What?"

"Are you DEAF?" shouts the pint-size Johnny Large. "When Johnny Large tells you to disrobe your clothes, your clothes had better start disrobing. Or do you boys want No Neck and Moose to disrobe yer clothes for you?"

Travis and Freddy shake their heads quickly and quietly say:

"No."

"Today is your lucky day, monkey boys. Today, you munchkins get a free lesson from the Johnny Large School of Hard Knocks, of which I am head perfessor and also top banana," he says with a sick twisted grin.

Two minutes and forty-eight seconds later, out on the balcony of the thirty-fifth floor, Travis and Freddy look painfully, pitifully pale in their tighty-whitey underpants, with their hairless, goose-pimpled, chicken-skinny legs quaking.

"Nice gams." The little Mr. Large laughs.

No Neck and Moose think this is genuinely funny and giggle like pumped-up 250-pound schoolgirls.

So now everybody's laughing, except the nearly naked Travis and Freddy.

And Sam, of course, who sits inside worried sick for our young heroes.

"Actually," says Freddy, "we wanted to take this opportunity to officially apologize, and . . ."

". . . and we'd be totally willing to just go home and forget the whole thing," Travis finishes.

"That brings us to Life Lesson number one at the Johnny Large School of Hard Knocks: Never let nobody make a monkey outta ya. Is that clear?" asks Johnny Large.

"Yes," mumble the bare-legged tighty-whitied boys.

"Repeat Lesson number one," says Johnny Large, "and also say it again."

"Never let nobody make a monkey outta ya," repeat Travis and Freddy.

"Excellent," says Johnny Large. "To ill-ustreate this point, I believe it would behoof you boys to start impersonating little monkeys. I think this will greatly enhance the edufication process."

Travis and Freddy look at each other, not sure exactly how to act like a monkey.

"Commence with being simian-type monkey," says

Johnny Large. "Scratch about under your arms, pound upon your chest, make with the ape sounds, and generally jump around like little monkey boys."

Travis and Freddy look at each other out of eye corners. They have put themselves in a position where they have no choice but to indulge this tiny madman.

So they scratch under their arms, pound chests with fists, make ape sounds, and jump around like little monkey boys.

"I do not feel you are exertating with maximum effort, or trying hard enough, do you, fellas?" Johnny Large asks Moose and No Neck.

"No," the muscle grunts.

So Travis and Freddy scratch, pound, jump, howl, and monkey-boy around even harder.

No Neck and Moose giggle again, and Johnny Large laughs loud. He's finally enjoying himself. His blood pressure drops.

Back in the suite, a tied-up Sam sees her dad dying in jail. This makes her think: I gotta do something. But what? she asks herself. I have no idea, she replies.

"We procede now to Life Lesson number two," says the compact Johnny Large. "If a fellow human tries to make a monkey outta you, you have two choices. One: Kill that human, preferably in a excrupillating manner and also slowly and painful. Two: Dangle that human off a very tall building. I will now display some of the classic Johnny Large generosity and ask you little monkey boys which option you'd prefer. Die. Or dangle. I see the dangle as a better option, as this way you do not buy the farm, kick the bucket, or die. As for me, I can rest assured that you will spread the word hither and yon that Johnny Large is a fierce yet reasonable fellow who is not to be monkeyed with under any circumstance. But the choice is yours. Die. Or dangle."

"Dangle," murmur Travis and Freddy, fear filling their eyes.

"Excellent choice." Johnny Large motions to No Neck and Moose.

Their meaty hands nab Travis and Freddy by the bands of the underpants and yank, resulting in industrial-strength wedgies.

"I believe, schooling-wise, it is our duty as Americans to take an interest in the education of today's youth," waxes Johnny Large. "They're our future, you know."

No Neck and Moose grab Travis and Freddy by the ankles and dangle them over the Vegas Strip, thirty-five floors up.

The boys try to scream. Nothing comes out but pure mute fear.

"Now make like you're flying, monkey boys," chirps Johnny Large. "Flap those little monkey wings. Fly, monkey boys, fly!"

A traumatized Travis and a fear-filled Freddy flap

their hands as best they can while hanging upside down thirty-five stories over the Vegas Strip in their tighty-whitey underpants.

"It is a jungle out there. Do you now see this from the position youze are in?" Johnny Large asks sarcastically. "And do you now capiche that Johnny Large is King of the Jungle, while you are pitiful little monkey boys?"

Hanging upside down, Travis and Freddy squeak:

"Yes."

From the street, where they were looking up less than twenty-four hours ago, the dangling boys look like tiny hanging wedgied-tighty-whitey-underpanted specks.

When the boys look down, the scurrying sidewalk gamblers look like little retired ant people.

"Perhaps I have erred on the side of nice," says Johnny Large. "Perhaps we *should* let these little monkey boys plummet to their death, and watch with glee as their little coconuts crack open and their brains spill on the sidewalk below."

Freddy sees himself and Travis falling falling falling in horror, unable to stop, knowing his big brain is going to be squeegeed off the Vegas pavement.

Travis sees his mom's sad face when she gets the news that her son is dead.

This makes him so sad that he says to the upside-down Freddy:

"I'm sorry."

To which the upside-down Freddy replies:

"Me, too."

The panic-packed boys try to look up and plead, but if you've ever been dangled by your ankles thirty-five stories up, you know that's not easy.

"Yes, I think we should revoke the dangle option. I believe, upon further retrospection, that the drop will be much more effective here, for purely edumacational purposes," the miniature Johnny Large barks. "Go ahead. Drop the little monkey boys."

Moose and No Neck release their grip on Travis and Freddy.

Travis and Freddy scream louder than they've ever screamed, knowing in less than ten seconds, their coconuts will be splattered on the sidewalk below.

They sound like this:

"¡¡¡AAAAAAAAAAAAAAAAAAAAAAAAAAAAAAAAAAAAAAAAAAAAAAAAAAAAAAAAAAAAAAAAAAAAAAAAW"

Johnny Large grins when he hears the boys scream.

Then just as quickly as they let go, Moose and No Neck grab the boys' ankles, saving them from becoming coconut milk.

"All right, bring the little monkey boys back up."

No Neck and Moose pull Travis and Freddy up and drop them back down on the balcony.

The boys shiver. Not because it's a cold night. Because

that's what you do when you're twelve, you're basically naked, and you just escaped a date with death by the seat of your tighty-whities.

Catching their breath, they follow Johnny Large and his muscle geeks back into the suite. Once inside, Johnny Large turns sharp and growls at Travis and Freddy. They jump back instinctively, shivering like whipped dogs. Johnny Large is having the time of his life. This is how he wants everyone to react when he turns sharp and growls at them. His blood pressure drops even lower.

"Leave my sight, never again darken my door, and also scram," says Johnny Large.

Travis and Freddy shoot Sam a what-do-we-do? look, and when she gives them a get-out-while-you-still-can, they grab their clothes to go.

"No, no, no." Johnny Large shakes his little head. "You are now ready for your final Life Lesson here at the Johnny Large School of Hard Knocks. When someone tries to make a monkey outta you, and you give them the dangle option, you convicate their clothes and expulse them out in their little monkey-boy underpants. Capiche?"

The boys nod their heads.

"I hope you reflect long and hard on what you have learned today. You can't buy this kind of edufication, my young monkey boys," says Johnny Large.

"I feel like I've learned a lot," Travis says earnestly.

"Yes, this *has* been very edu . . . ficational," Freddy says sincerely.

"And what have you learned today from Perfessor Johnny Large?" Johnny Large smiles.

"That Johnny Large is the King of the Jungle," says Travis.

"Precisely." Johnny Large smiles. "Continue."

"And if anybody tries to make a monkey out of us—" Travis says.

"We should either kill them or dangle them off a balcony in their underpants," says Freddy.

"Then take their clothes away," says Travis.

"And most importantly, Johnny Large is a very dangerous but very generous—" says Freddy.

"And extremely handsome man," finishes Travis.

"So true. Youze are excellent students, and youze have learnt your lessons with extreme ineptitude. Class dismissed. And let me assure you that if I ever lay eyes on your ugly monkey-boy mugs again, Johnny Large will be the last thing you ever see! And your graduation privileges will be rebuked permanently on account of you all of a sudden coming down with a bad case of being dead."

Travis and Freddy nod, knowing this is their cue to vamoose, which is another word for "scram."

They stare at Sam again. They don't want to leave

her behind. They believe it's all their fault that she's tied to a chair in the suite of her worst enemy.

But there's absolutely nothing they can do about it.

Sam smiles a tiny smile to let them know it's okay. Even though everyone knows it's not okay. Then she jerks her head ever so slightly, signaling for the boys to go. Now!

As they walk out wearing nothing but their wounded pride and their tighty-whities, the boys are sure they'll never see Sam again. And it's breaking their almost-thirteen-year-old hearts.

Skinny Fists, a Dripping Pencil & Dried Blood

U ntil you've done it, you have no idea how bad it is to be waiting for an elevator in a hotel hallway when you've just lost the money to save your family, left your new friend in a gangster's lair, and you're in your tiny tighty-whitey underpants.

The elevator will take forever. That's what it's doing now to Travis and Freddy. Making them wait in their pitiful humiliation.

Travis, desperate for someone to blame, turns to Freddy and says:

"Well, I hope you're happy."

For a second, Freddy thinks maybe he's having an ear hallucination because he's so upset. So he says:

"What did you say?"

"I. Hope. You're. Happy," Travis snarls.

Freddy believes his ears now. Which leads his mouth to say:

"What's that supposed to mean?"

"You know exactly what that means." Travis is full of mean and ugly.

"No, I don't." Freddy's getting quite steamed up. "Why don't you explain it to me."

"This was all your stupid idea," Travis barks. "If it wasn't for you, Sam wouldn't be in there about to get—"

"Wait a minute, hold on a second, if it wasn't for your stupid deadbeat old man, we wouldn't be here in the first place!" screams Freddy, hitting the lowest of blows.

"Take it back!" Travis snaps.

"No!" shouts Freddy.

"Take it back!" Travis pushes Freddy.

"No!" Freddy pushes back.

"You BETTER take it BACK!" Travis shoves Freddy harder.

"NO!" Freddy shoves Travis harder than he's ever shoved anyone before.

"TAKE IT BACK!" Travis makes a hard fist.

Cocks the fist.

Swings it as hard as he can at Freddy.

The fist hits Freddy in the side of his head.

CRACK!

Freddy's big brain snaps back.

It doesn't hurt yet. But it will. Right now Freddy's head is too stunned to hurt.

Travis has threatened to punch him 247 times in the last twelve years, eleven months, and twenty-five days. But he's never done it. Until now.

Freddy has been getting pushed around his whole life. He's so tired of it that something now snaps inside him, and he lower his just-punched brain-packed cranium, thrust it down and forward, runs as fast as he can, and rams right into the belly of Travis.

Direct hit. Travis's feet fly up, and he sails back, landing with a sliding, thumping thud. Freddy pounces on Travis. His body takes over, and all it wants to do is pummel Travis, so his fists windmill ferociously, raining blows all over Travis.

Travis grabs Freddy's shoulders and tries to yank his best friend off. But he can't stop those skinny fists from slamming into his handsome, perfectly formed nose.

CRACK! SLAM! BAM!

It doesn't hurt yet. But it will. Travis feels warm and wet on his face. Blood. His own blood. This make Travis so furious he flings Freddy off with a great grunt, and in the process his elbow slams smack-dab into Freddy's mouth.

CRUNCH!

Freddy feels wet and warm on his face. Blood. His own blood.

Travis and Freddy pull back from the frenzy and take a good look at each other. When each sees the bloody mess they've made of the other, hostilities immediately cease.

"You're bleeding," says Travis.

"So are you," says Freddy.

Pause. Together they say:

"Sorry."

The elevator dings, and when the doors slide open, several retirees eye the suddenly startled, nearly naked Travis and Freddy. When it's clear the boys aren't really hurt, the geezer gamblers cackle with mad laughs.

Travis and Freddy feel their faces go red, like they're boiling from the inside. They don't know it, but it's a different shade of red than the blood trickling out of their nose and mouth respectively.

The most horrible day of their lives just got worse. The elevator door slowly shuts, mercifully muffling the mockery directed at the bloodied and bowed Travis and Freddy.

Just as the boys are sure their geese are finally fully cooked, a man they recognize rounds the corner.

It's Carl.

He's been worried about Travis and Freddy all alone and on their own in Vegas, and he's coming to check up on them. He's unaware of the goofy-magic-glasses-gambling episode, the All You Can Eat food-fight fiasco, or the underpanted dangling. He has no idea Sam is tied up in the suite of Johnny Large. And he certainly does not expect to see the boys in the hall wearing tighty-whities and bloody faces. After he studies them up and down, he says:

"Jeez Louise, what the heck happened to the Glimmer Twins?"

Travis and Freddy don't even know where to start, so they shrug, sigh, and try not to cry.

"Let's get you back to your room, and you can tell me all about it." Carl pities the quivering lads.

"Are You Lonesome Tonight?" plays as he lets the boys back into the Elvis Suite and says to them:

"You boys seen Sam?"

Travis and Freddy look at each other with twin terror.

"What's goin' on? Where's Sam?" Carl demands. "Start talkin', NOW!"

Two hundred and four yards away, in his own thirty-fifth-floor suite, Johnny Large says to Sam:

"Start talkin', NOW!"

While Travis and Freddy spill their sad-sack story to Carl, Johnny Large bores in on Sam, trying to crack her nut, as he's cracked so many before her.

Carl shakes his angry head while phoning to get clothes for the boys. After he hangs up, he turns and says with severe gravity:

"Do NOT!!! Leave. This. Room. DO YOU UNDER-STAND?"

As Carl storms off to rescue Sam, Travis and Freddy

nod like puppies just smacked on their wet noses, then sink into their misery.

Back in tiny Johnny Large's huge suite, he picks up an apple in one hand and a way-sharp pencil in the other. He walks in small slow circles around the bound Sam.

"When I was a young buck," says little Johnny Large, "there was this wisenheimer, this real cute operator, and one day he was walking around with a pencil of the . . . sharp variety."

Try as she might, Sam can't keep her eyes off the way-sharp pencil point in the miniature hand of Johnny Large.

"Well, he was quite careless, and also not paying attention, and he tripped something terrible." Johnny Large chuckles. "Can you imagine what happened next?"

"Uh, lemme think. Did the pencil accidentally get jammed up your nose, thus stunting your growth and leaving you a physical and mental midget?" Sam says with as much attitude as she can muster.

Johnny Large growls and brings the pencil just to the tip of Sam's left eyeball.

"WRONG ANSWER!!! What happened was, this particular wise guy," Johnny Large says between clenched teeth, "he got a pencil of the very sharp variety jammed right through his eyeball!"

Johnny Large jams the way-sharp pencil into the apple, clear through to the other side, and an apple-juice teardrop drips down the pencil.

Please don't flinch, Sam begs herself as she flinches.

This makes a cool calm come over Johnny Large while his blood pressure swan-dives, and he says:

"I would hate to see your pretty little eyeball have a pencil punctuate it, so why do you not now tell me from where I know you from?"

"Honest," lies Sam, "we've never met before—"

"Do not deceive, decease, or otherwise lie to me. Have you not seen what happens to people who try to make a monkey out of Johnny Large? Disrobe the glasses off her," barks Johnny Large.

Back in the Elvis Suite, Freddy, who is looking for the magic old-lady glasses, realizes Sam still has them, and turns on the big TV. No Neck's cinder-block-size head fills the screen when he leans in and removes the glasses. The contents of the room turn upside down as he puts the glasses upside down on the table next to Sam.

Sam seems to sit on the ceiling as a tiny upside-down Johnny Large eases the dripping pencil out of the wounded upside-down apple.

The boys, awash in horror, pace, picking dried blood from their faces, as Freddy tries to figure out what to do, while Travis repeats:

"My dad's gonna kill me.

"My dad's gonna kill me.

"My dad's gonna kill me."

Until finally Freddy can't stand it anymore and says: "Will you stop saying that?"

"Sorry," says Travis.

Back to pacing.

Travis says again:

"But my dad's gonna kill me—"

Freddy stops him by yelling:

"STOP!"

"We should call my folks," says Travis.

"And tell them what? We're in Vegas, we're busted, and we're in our underpants?" Freddy demands.

"Good point. Guess not." Travis's brain turns once again into warm lumpy tapioca pudding. "What *are* we gonna tell our folks?"

"We gotta do the honorable thing," says Freddy.

"What's that?" asks Travis.

"Lie," says Freddy.

"Right," says Travis.

Another tiny event changes everything. When Johnny Large jerks the dripping pencil point toward Sam's eyeball, she instinctively snaps her head back, and her wig moves.

"Well, well, well, what have we here?" Johnny Large muses. He yanks Sam's wig off and studies her closely, a giant evil grin spreading across his bitter little face.

As the boys turn their attention to the upside-down, about-to-be-killed Sam, they stop caring about anything except helping her.

"All is now clear to me." Johnny Large breathes in relief, like when you remove a troubling splinter from your foot. "It's the wise-guy child of that moronical idiot I sent to the slammer."

No Neck and Moose grunt agreeably.

"Oh my, but this will be amusing, and also lots of fun." Johnny Large drips glee.

The boys' skin crawls.

"You're a lot shorter and more hideous than I remember," says Sam.

Johnny Large's blood pressure pumps up, and a hideous grimace takes up residence on his mean face.

Travis and Freddy can't stop themselves from imagining Sam with the very sharp pencil sticking out of her eyeball, and it fills them with deep dread. Because they know in their almost-thirteen-year-old hearts that they are responsible.

Johnny Large sees the same thing, but it fills him with glee and makes his blood pressure plunge.

"What a mouth you have," Johnny Large spits at Sam. "A mouth such as this could land a person in a pickle, a pinch, and a jam, not to mention also possibly in a severe state of being dead."

Sam's brain crashes. When it reboots, the screen saver

on the inside of her mind's eye is a picture she's seen a thousand times before: her dad being released from prison, throwing his arms triumphantly around her, and hugging her like he never wants to let go.

All of this is interrupted by something no one expected. A knock on the door of Johnny Large's suite. By a man who stands in the hallway of the thirty-fifth floor in a huge stupid feathery hat, pointy shoes, cheesy green tights, and a ruffled shirt, next to a fully loaded room-service tray.

Caviar, a Purple Dinosaur, & the Geek Greek Chorus

ohnny Large shrugs from his inner sanctum and tosses a glance at No Neck. No Neck shrugs. Which is not easy when you have no neck. He turns to the clueless Moose, who shrugs, too. He and No Neck reach their hands under their jackets and finger the triggers of their guns.

Johnny Large motions for No Neck to answer the door. No Neck trundles thick out of the Master Suite, then says to the door:

"Who is it?"

"Room service," comes from the other side.

No Neck crunches back into the Master Suite and looks at Johnny Large, who shakes his head and mouths:

"No."

No Neck galumphs back to the door and says, "We didn't order no room service."

"Compliments of Mr. Wayne Newton," comes through the door.

"Compliments of Mr. Wayne Newton," No Neck shouts back to Large.

"Oh, I did not realize Wayne was back in town. It appears he is resuscitating my frequent attempts at friendship. Is it caviar and champagne?" asks Johnny Large. He doesn't even like caviar and champagne, but because they're the most expensive things on the room-service menu, they make him happy.

"Is it caviar and champagne?" asks No Neck.

"Yes, it is," comes back.

"Yeah, it is," No Neck yells back.

"Bring it on," yells Johnny Large from the Master Suite.

No Neck opens the door.

Carl smiles and rolls the cart in. As he enters the Master Suite, No Neck stops him.

"I'll take this," says No Neck.

"Sure, just let me get the ice out." Carl grins as he reaches under the cart, which is covered by a tablecloth.

Instead of ice, Carl pulls out a gun, while the other hand flashes a badge at No Neck, then motions for him to keep quiet.

He marches No Neck to the doorway of the Master Suite, throws Sam a Prince-Charming's-here-to-save-the-day look, eyeballs little Johnny Large, and proclaims:

"FBI. You're under arrest for kidnapping. You have the right to remain silent . . . you have the right to consult an attorney . . . If you cannot afford an attorney—"

Johnny Large bursts out laughing, his blood pressure plummeting again.

When Johnny Large laughs like that, Carl suspects his plan has gone awry. When he looks out the corner of his eye and sees the barrel of the enormous gun Moose is pointing at his head, he knows he's right.

"My, but I love those tights." Johnny Large laughs. "They really showcase your gams."

Moose and No Neck giggle.

"Nice rod." Johnny Large chuckles with a smirk at Carl's gun. "Where'd you get it, a Cracker Jack box?"

No Neck and Moose giggle harder. Suddenly Carl's thinking maybe this wasn't such a great plan after all. He looks at Sam. She rolls her eyes. Carl feels like as huge a fool as he looks.

"That's All Right, Mama" plays in the Elvis Suite as Travis and Freddy go from horrified to out-of-their-minds.

"We *gotta* do something," says Travis.

"We gotta *do* something," says Freddy. "Can you believe Carl's with the feds?"

"I can't believe Carl's with the feds," says Travis.

"Unbelievable," says Freddy.

"Who are the feds again?" asks Travis.

"The FBI," says Freddy.

"Right," says Travis. "That's amazing, from room service to FBI in one day."

"He's undercover, bobblehead," says Freddy.

"Ohhhhh, undercover," says Travis. "Cooooool."

Freddy thinks for one minute and twelve seconds. Then he says:

"I got it."

Travis doesn't argue. This time he jumps into action, and together they throw loads of supplies into backpacks.

In Johnny Large's suite, No Neck pockets Carl's gun. This makes the little gangster man happier than he's been in a long time. He says:

"For years I have believed you were a nincompoop and also an idiot. It is nice to see I was correct."

Pause for laugh. Geek Greek chorus of No Neck and Moose obliges with dumb chuckles.

"Hey, Mr. FBI, did you really think you could just waltz into the house of Johnny Large, wave your pitiful little thingy around, and take me down? Do you not know who Johnny Large is? Moose, remind Carl now of who Johnny Large is."

Moose smashes Carl's head with his gun butt. Carl crumbles crashing to the floor, where he does a remarkable impression of a sack full of potatoes.

Sam winces

What fun! Johnny Large grins wickedly. Not just the daughter of an old enemy, but a fed to boot.

No Neck kicks Carl in the stomach with the steel hidden under the wing tip of his shoe.

Three of Carl's ribs crack. It feels like hot knives are

stabbing into his guts, as this sound whomps out of him:

"Awwwwwwwowwwwwwwohhhhhahhhhhh."

This will make it hard for Carl to do many things, such as laughing, sneezing, and breathing, as he finds out now when he tries to breathe and his ribs scream at him furiously.

Johnny Large, on the other hand, finds it very easy to laugh in the face of Carl's pain, and he does so now. When the laugh dies, he says:

"Tie these two stooges together. I cannot help myself, I am a hopeless romantical."

Upside down on the big screen in the Elvis Suite, No Neck and Moose throw a pain-racked Carl upside down into a chair and tie him back-to-back to the upside-down Sam, while Freddy prints out the floor plan for the thirty-fifth floor and Travis takes the screen off the air-conditioning vent.

"Ready?" says Freddy.

"Ready, Freddy," says Travis.

Carl desperately wants to look into Sam's eyes, but when he tries to twist, a fiery agony attacks his cracked ribs and his breath vanishes.

"Nice job," Sam spits sarcastically through her teeth.

"Look," Carl hisses through his hurt, "if we could just—"

"There is no we," says Sam. "There's you and there's me, and I've had more than enough of you."

"But what is this? A lovers' spat? True love is so hard to find, is it not?" Johnny Large asks No Neck and Moose.

"Definitely," they grunt, though they know nothing of true love.

"Did you ever hear the story of Romeo and Juliet?" asks Johnny Large. "These are a couple of young losers who find true love. I cannot recall all the impertinent details, but I seem to rememberate that they croak, buy the farm, and die like miserable dogs. If I am not mistooken, I believe they get buried alive in the Vegas desert, do they not?"

"Yeah," says Moose.

"I think so," says No Neck.

Sam and Carl see themselves buried alive, mouths sucking sand, lungs suffocating.

Travis Best and Freddy Quigley, strapped to supply-filled backpacks, are currently crawling through the air-conditioning duct on the thirty-fifth floor, from the Elvis Suite to the monster suite of the tiny sourball Johnny Large.

As the boys pass a duct, they look into the room and spy a guy dressed as a big purple dinosaur, talking to a fat man in a too-tight suit. Either the suit's too small, or the man's too big.

"If I have to sing "I Love You, You Love Me" one more time, I'm gonna puke," says the man dressed as the purple dinosaur, who seems like he'd enjoy punching the fat man in the too-tight suit.

Travis and Freddy crawl by another duct, past a room full of Elvis impersonators stuffing their faces with fat-filled foods of all shapes, sizes, and colors.

When finally the boys reach the elevator shaft, Lady Luck smiles on them, and the elevator is there, like a land bridge connecting Russia and Alaska. Without the elevator being in exactly the right place, they could never have crossed to the next duct.

Travis smiles as he walks easily across the top of the elevator to the air-conditioning shaft on the other side.

Freddy smiles as he follows Travis across the top of the elevator.

"Piece of pie," says Travis.

"Piece of cake, ya mukluk," says Freddy.

"What's mukluk again?" Travis asks, stepping off the top of the elevator and into the air-conditioning shaft.

"Eskimo footwear," replies Freddy.

Lady Luck now departs as the elevator jolts to life and start to zoom up, taking Freddy with it.

Freddy, never the calmest of fellows, plunges into panic, falling in a heap on top of the elevator, as it flies up fast.

"Freddy, you okay?" yells Travis, trying not to sound as scared as he is.

"No," yells Freddy, sounding every bit as scared as he is.

Travis and Freddy have the same vision:

They see Freddy crushed into the ceiling, turned into a smushed, mushed, pulpy bloody mess. So he lies flat on the top of the elevator as it flies upupup, and blows out as much breath as he can, trying to turn himself into a one-dimensional line drawing. When he looks up and sees the ceiling zooming at his head, terror takes his face hostage. Freddy knows he's going to die, and the last thing his big brain thinks is: We're not gonna get to save Sam now.

Freddy sadly closes his eyes to die. He wishes he'd said good-bye to his dad and told Travis what a cool guy he is. He hopes there is a heaven and that his mom is waiting for him there with freshly baked chocolate-chip cookies.

In the horrible silence, all Travis can see is Freddy's guts spread all over the concrete ceiling like twelve-year-old jelly.

"Freeeeeeeeeddddyyyyyyyyyyyyyyy!" Trav's voice shakes, his heart breaking.

He knows his best friend is dead. Sadness overpowers him, 'cuz he didn't ever get to tell Freddy what a cool guy he is.

But Death is once more denied, for when the ceiling gets 5.7 inches from Freddy's long nose, the elevator stops. Freddy sniffs the concrete. It has no smell at all. And not one bit of Freddy's big brain is gooed on it.

"Freddy? You okay?" Travis yells tentatively up the shaft.

When Freddy hears Trav's voice, more familiar than his own, he feels even happier to be alive and realizes once again how lucky he is to have the one and only Travis Best as his best friend.

"I think so," Freddy squeaks.

When Travis hears Freddy's voice, he realizes once again how lucky he is to have the one and only Freddy Quigley as his best friend.

Suddenly the elevator jolts to life and starts sliding back down toward Travis.

"When the elevator stops here, just jump right into the shaft with me. Okay?" asks Travis.

"Okay," says Freddy. "Trav?"

"Yeah," says Travis.

"What if the elevator doesn't stop at thirty-five?" Freddy asks as the elevator begins zooming down.

"If it doesn't stop here, I'll grab you as it goes by, and I'll pull ya in," says Travis, who believes with all his heart that Freddy can do it.

"I can't," says Freddy, who believes with all his heart that he can't.

"Sure ya can," says Travis.

"No Trav, I can't," says Freddy as the elevator jolts past the thirty-sixth floor.

"You can, man," says Trav. "Besides, it'll probably stop here anyway."

"Yeah probably," Freddy says, even though he doesn't believe it.

Freddy sees himself grabbing Travis's hand, dangling down the shaft, hanging on to Travis's hand for dear life, then losing his grip and plunging downdowndown, exploding like an egg on the roof of the elevator twenty-five stories below, guts splattering everywhere.

He tries putting that picture in the trash on the desktop of his mind and attempts to empty it. Somehow it ends up as his screen saver.

Freddy's heart and stomach jump together into his mouth as the elevator plunges down.

"I can't—" cranks out of his mouth.

"Sure you can," says Travis.

"No, I can't," cries Freddy.

"How old are you?" Travis shouts.

Nothing comes back as the elevator comes zooming down.

"How old are you?" Travis yells again.

The elevator's bottom sizzles past Travis, showing no signs of slowing.

Freddy's bottom now joins his stomach and his heart in his mouth, which tries to scream. Unfortunately, it's too crowded in there, and nothing comes out.

The top of the elevator is now even with the top of the

air-conditioning duct. The boys know the moment of decision is upon them, but it's all happening so fast, they can hardly keep up.

Travis sees Freddy's feet, crouched and ready to leap.

"HOW OLD ARE YOU?" Travis screams.

Freddy meets Travis's eyes, and this makes his arms reach for Trav, his legs spring forward, and his feet push off, while his mouth yells:

"THIRRRTEEEEEEEEEN!"

As the elevator flies down, Travis grabs Freddy's left hand. Freddy's right hand grabs Travis's shirt. Travis pulls on Freddy while Freddy pulls on Travis.

They hang there, rocking between disaster and safety. Paused poised between up and down. Between Salvation and Doom. Gravity pulls. Balance shifts.

Freddy unintentionally starts to pull his best friend down the shaft with him. And as he clings to Travis, like he has all his life, they begin to drop down toward the hard roof of the elevator so far below.

Freddy looks into Travis's eyes. If they have to die, at least they're doing it together.

But Travis Best doesn't hit last-second baskets by accident. When everything's on the line, and people all around him are losing their heads, that's when everything goes slow motion for Travis.

Anchored in the shaft, he realizes that if he grabs Freddy by the seat of the pants, he can pull his best friend back up into the shaft with him.

So Travis very calmly does just that.

Freddy falls smack-dab on Trav, who lands with a whack on his back. His long nose is now up against Travis's perfect one. Which is much better than ceiling concrete.

Freddy smiles as he says:

"Thanks, man."

Travis smiles as he says:

"Don't mention it."

"Man, you got some serious dog breath," says Freddy.

"Well, you got serious Raptor-armpit breath," says Travis.

"GROOOOOOOOOOOOOOOOOOOOOOOOOOOOOOSSSS!!!" echoes merrily through the elevator shaft of the Excalibur Hotel and Casino.

A Stink, Doodly-Squat & Romance Croaking

I need a couple of packages taken care of," No Neck mumbles with a grunt. "Immediately . . . Yeah, to Area 54. Right. Two packages. Twenty minutes? Perfect."

Sam and Carl, who are the packages, fill with desperate terror and again have the same vision: buried alive, sand in the ears eyes nose and throat choking with sand, lungs gulping for air, dying with maximum horror.

"Many say in this cynical age of jadiosity that romance has croaked," proclaims Johnny Large. "'Ha!' says I. When I think of these two star-crossed lovers buried together in the sands of eternity, it reminds me again of Juliet and Romeo, who also bit the dust with such romanticality."

"Let her go, she didn't do anything," says Carl, even though he knows there's no way that's going to happen, in this lifetime or the next.

"Drop dead," says Sam, who knows a hollow gesture when she sees one.

"It wasn't my fault," says Carl. "I did everything—"

"You sold out my old man," says Sam. "End of story."

"Ahhhhhhh, now I am seeing the reason for this lovers' spat," says Johnny Large with a malicious little grin. "Well, Johnny Large will now set the record straight so the lovers can die a truly stupid death with great tragicality."

"What are you talking about?" asks Sam.

"Mr. Fed here"—Johnny Large points his little hand at Carl—"has zero, zilch, bubkes, beans, diddly, doodly-squat, and also nothing to do with your old man getting yacked. You have only Johnny Large to thank for that. Leave no good deed unpunished, says I. Let me explain further and also more. You see, your old man"—he points to Sam—"was prepared to rat me out to your fed boyfriend here, and that would be extremely negatory for Johnny Large. So you can see he left me no choice but to set him up and cook him like a goose. In fact, I happen to know that Señor Fed here busted his hump trying to get your old man cleared. Fortunately, I knows certain other humanaries in the FBI, such as the big kahuna of the Vegas district, who happens to owe me many favors both big and huge. Is that not correct, boys?"

"Huge," grunts Mr. Large's muscle, "and big."

"So you see," continues Johnny Large, "the G-man's love for you was true. It is not him, but rather Johnny

Large, who deserves your unending disrespect and hatred, which, unfortunately, will have to end in about half an hour when you have become dead."

"Is that true?" says Sam.

"Of course it is; that's what I've been trying to tell you for a year," says Carl.

Sam tries to digest this startling piece of news. Then she says:

"Sorry, sometimes I can be a real horse's patoot."

Carl tries to smile, but it hurts too much.

"Do you not find true love beautiful?" Johnny Large grins with grim satisfaction. "Especially when it dies buried alive in the Vegas desert."

"Oh yeah," answer No Neck and Moose, because they know they're supposed to.

KAPLOWIE!

An explosion of sound.

ZIP! ZING! ZONG!

Smoke thick and stinky fills the room.

Whap! Whack! Wham!

No Neck, Moose, and Johnny Large are hit hard in the head, thumped in the throat, and pelted heavily.

KAPLOWIE!

Lights flash and machine-gun sounds rattle:

rat-a-tat-tat!

Johnny Large has dreamed for many years that he would be gunned down by someone he's abused, ripped off, or humiliated. He's sure his nightmare is coming true at this very moment when he feels a bullet hit his neck, and he sees red blood when he touches his hand to the wound.

KAPLOWIE!

Johnny Large crumbles, imagining a handsome movie star playing him in the movie version of his life.

No Neck has dreamed for many years that when Johnny Large is finally gunned down in a blaze of glory, he will utterly humiliate himself by turning into a quivering cowardly mass of steroid-fueled jelly. As he feels a bullet hit him in the chest and sees red blood coming from his wound, No Neck crumbles, transformed into a quivering cowardly mass of steroid-fueled jelly.

Meanwhile, Moose moves wildly through the confusion yelling:

"I don't wanna die!

"I don't wanna die!

"I don't wanna die!"

They have no idea that they've actually been hit with cherries from a slingshot. Or that the machine gun/smoke/explosions are actually part GameStation, part firecracker, part sparkler, and part stink bomb.

And, of course, they have no idea that Travis and Freddy have removed the grate from the air-conditioning duct and are inside it, gleefully responsible for all the chaos and mayhem.

Freddy nudges Travis. Loads up a cherry in his slingshot. Takes aim at Johnny Large's minuscule coconut. Let's her fly.

DIRECT HIT!

Believing he is dying, little Johnny Large grabs his tiny temple, crawls into a ball, and bawls like a baby:

"WAAAAAAAAAAAAAAAAAAAAAAAAAAAAAAA!"

Travis looks at Freddy, puts a thumb up, and smiles his million-dollar smile.

Freddy looks at Travis, puts a thumb up, and feels like a million bucks.

Stink bombs pump foul funk into the air. Smoke detectors activate:

BEEP! BEEP! BEEP! BEEP! BEEP! BEEP!

Sprinklers rain on the parade of Johnny Large, soaking all to the bone.

Carl uses all the wet, smoky, noisy, stinky confusion to violently twist the chairs he and Sam are tied to. This makes these things happen:

Sam topples on top of Carl. Carl's busted ribs are body-slammed by Sam. Carl's face plants into the carpeted floor, smashing his nose, which explodes with blood. He lands hard and crooked on his arm, snapping his wrist bone. Pain e-mails to Carl's brain, which downloads it and screams as quiet as it can:

"Yeeeeeeeeoowwwwwwww!"

Sam feels terrible for Carl and tries to wriggle them free. But every time she does, a brutal new stab shoots through him.

Sam yanks her left hand free. She finds the end of the rope, pulls it through a knot, unties herself, then does the same for Carl.

Johnny Large sees a maraschino cherry next to him on the carpet. This is when he first suspects he's not going to die quite yet. He touches his neck. No bullet hole. Only cherry juice. As Johnny Large rises he wonders: What the heck is going on here?

Sam has just helped Carl up. His nose is smashed,

wrist broken, and three ribs are cracked, but apart from that, he's never felt better in his life.

Johnny Large and Sam suddenly stand face-to-face. When she looks into his eyes, Sam knows exactly what to do. She rears back with her right foot and brings it up very hard between Mr. Large's little legs as she says:

"This one's for my old man!"

As they watch Sam's high-top make contact with the most private tiny area of Johnny Large, Travis and Freddy smile and golf-clap. When Johnny Large crashes like a sock puppet, Sam and Carl grin at each other.

Having heard the alarm, the firecrackers, and the machine gun, and having seen the smoke creepy-crawling out under the door, Glenn Peabody, a security guard who's shot three people, opens the door and leads J. D. Russell and Chris Bodine, two security guards who've never shot anyone, into the room. They're expecting Trouble. Guns drawn, fingers twitching, itching, and tingling, they try to make sense of what they see through the thick stinky clouds and sprinkler rain.

Johnny Large crumpled in agony on the wet carpet.

A happily drenched woman holding up a bloody man who is laughing and grimacing simultaneously.

A huge brute quivering on the floor.

A huge Moose whimpering while waving, scurrying, and screaming: "I don't want to die."

They don't, of course, see the two practically-thirteen-year-old boys who survey the whole thing like triumphant yet anonymous heroes from inside the air-conditioning duct.

The law enforcement personnel simultaneously regain their sense of smell.

"What stinks?" Glenn verbalizes for all of them.

"Him," says Sam as she points to the small fallen Johnny Large.

Travis and Freddy chuckle.

Carl starts to laugh, but immediately stops because it hurts too much. Grimacing gingerly, he flashes his badge and hisses:

"Carl Sears, FBI. Book these three: extortion, racketeering, kidnapping, conspiracy to commit murder—we'll start there, and see where it takes us."

"You want us to book Johnny Large?" J. D. squeaks incredulously.

"This is an OUT-RAGE of the most magnanimous proportions—" Johnny Large starts.

Carl cuts him off colder than a tongue stuck to a frozen pole:

"Shut up, little man."

Johnny Large is shocked silent. But not for long.

"You got no warrant, you got no proof, and by the time I get through with you, you're gonna wish you are only dead!" says the tiny Johnny Large with a snarling half smile.

"Large threatened to kill me. Carl, he just saved my life," says Sam, pointing at the sore Carl.

"You got no proof of nothing." Johnny Large is so mad he's practically dancing. "Plus, furthermore—"

"Helloooooooooooooooo!"

. . . floats in like cool air from the air-conditioning duct. All heads turn. Four twelve-year-old eyes stare out like jailbirds about to be sprung from the slammer.

Sam and Carl burst out laughing. Carl regrets it instantly and intensely.

"Of course, it's the Glimmer Twins outta Walla Walla!" says Sam happily. "I shoulda known."

"What are you boys . . . how did you do—" Carl stops because it seems pointless to go on.

Glenn the guard whips around, points his gun at the boys, and moves menacingly toward them.

"Put that away." Carl winces. "They're with me."

"Thanks," Sam whispers with a wink as she helps Travis and Freddy out of the air-conditioning duct.

"No problem." Travis trots out that million-dollar smile, while Freddy nods appreciatively.

"Hey, Carl," says Freddy, "how ya doin'?"

"I can't tell you how happy I am to see you guys again." Carl, trying not to breathe, gives them as much of a handshake as he can.

The sprinklers shut off, but the smell of doused firecracker and stink bomb hang heavy in the air.

TRAVIS & FREDDY

Travis and Freddy just can't stop grinning.

Johnny Large's blood pressure jumps, and it feels like a hammer is pounding a nail into his chest. Makes him want to watch everyone in the whole room die slowly and painfully. He desperately searches for the geese over the pond. But when he finally visualizes them, they attack him viciously, biting chunks out of his little head.

"You kids are gonna pay for this with—" Johnny Large starts.

"Ooooooooooooooooooooooh," Travis and Freddy cut him off, mimicking terror. "We're soooooooooooooo-oooooo scared."

"Yeah, he's such a tough guy," says Freddy. "You shoulda seen him crying like a baby—"

"WAAAAAAAA!" Travis does a perfect impression of Johnny Large wailing.

Everybody cracks up.

Except Johnny Large, of course.

Carl stops laughing quickly, 'cause it hurts too much.

"Lesson number one: Never let anyone make a monkey of you," says Freddy.

Travis and Sam smile. Johnny Large's blood pressure hits an air pocket and jumps straight up as he snarls:

"You ain't got nuthin' on me, ya little pipsqueaks. I'm innocent, and also not guilty, and if I was youze—"

"Well, you're not me, 'cause I happen to have the"

197

whole thing on videotape back in the room," says Freddy.

"You what?" says Carl.

"You what?" says Glenn.

"You what?" says Sam.

"You what?" says Johnny Large.

"Huh?" grunt Moose and No Neck.

"We videotaped the whole thing," says Travis. "It was Freddy's idea. He's a genius—"

"Thanks, Trav." Freddy smiles.

"Sure, Freddy." Trav smiles.

"We got some kidnapping, some fight fixing, a little extortion, conspiracy to commit murder," says Freddy.

"Plus planning to kill somebody, and tying people up, and being a nasty little troll," says Travis.

This makes Freddy laugh so hard he starts snorting, which makes Sam laugh really hard, which makes Carl laugh. Sadly, his assortment of broken, bruised, and bent body parts make the following sound leak out of him:

"Hhhhhhhhhhhmphhhhowwwwwwww."

"How did you do this?" asks Glenn.

Travis picks up the old-lady cat-eye glasses and says to Freddy:

"Tell him."

"A microscopic fiber-optic digital-signal processor

mini-microphonic transducer is planted here. A refractive receiver is here. I feed 'em into the supercomputer, and voilà, it's showtime," Freddy says in a voice deeper than it's ever been. Everyone nods their impressed heads.

"He's a genius," Sam and Travis say together.

Glenn is more or less dumbfounded. When he finally speaks, he says:

"How old are you kids, anyway?"

"They're thirteen," says Sam.

"Huh." Glenn looks at the boys hard, trying to make the whole thing compute.

Johnny Large, fully cuffed, tenses and clenches as his blood pressure rips into the red zone and sweat pours down his flaming cheeks, while his eyes look like little balls of fire that need to be put out.

Everything gets quiet, all eyes upon him, waiting for him to say something cruel, horrible, and nasty.

Johnny Large opens his mouth to say something cruel, horrible, and nasty.

But his wires are all crossed, his signals mixed, his mainframe fragmented, the motherboard overloaded, and as a result, this comes out:

"   ."

Nothing but dead air.

"Ya catch flies like that," Freddy says just loud enough.

Sam, Travis, the guards, even Carl—they all laugh.

Freddy basks in the fact that finally everyone is laughing *with* him instead of *at* him.

As Johnny Large, Moose, and No Neck are carted away by the guards, Sam, Travis, and Freddy wave at them like Miss Americas while they yell:

"Nice doing business with you!"

And:

"Bye, Tiny!"

And:

"Have fun in prison!"

Carl stops laughing and says:

"Ouch!" then grins with a grimace.

"We gotta get you to a hospital," Sam says to Carl.

"Yeah," says Travis, "we gotta take off, too. . . ."

"We gotta lotta stuff to, you know . . . take care of. . . ." says Freddy.

"Tons of stuff . . . so, uh . . . see you later," says Travis.

"Keep in touch," says Freddy.

Very casually Travis picks up the cash-filled Boy Scout satchel, Freddy picks up the old-lady glasses, and they try to ease out the door without anyone noticing.

Doesn't even come close to working.

"Whoa there, hold on a second," says Carl. "Where you two goin'?"

"Oh, well . . ." says Freddy.

"Yeah, uh . . ." adds Travis.

"What's in the bag?" asks Carl.

"What bag?" ask Travis and Freddy, their lame attempt at innocence fooling no one.

"The bag in your hand," says Carl.

"That's my bag, actually," says Sam, who grabs the bag that Travis holds.

Travis won't let go, though, so he and Sam stand there playing a $249,000 game of tug-of-war.

Carl stops the game with this:

"Gimme the bag. Now."

Travis and Sam reluctantly give Carl the bag.

When Carl looks in it, his mouth drops open and he starts to whistle, but stops because it hurts.

"What's in the bag?" asks Glenn, curious as only a frustrated security-guard guy can be.

This moment hangs there for a long time.

Travis looks at Freddy.

The boys look at Sam.

Sam and the boys look at Carl.

Carl looks from them, to the money, to Glenn.

Then he thinks for quite some time.

Travis and Freddy hold their breath, waiting to see if they'll be saved or busted.

Sam remembers why she used to like Carl so much.

Finally, he knows what to do. So he says:

"Oh, these are just some personal effects. I'll take care of it, you take care of the bad guys."

"Carl," says Glenn. "You want me to call you an ambulance?"

"No, I can get a cab," says Carl as he glances at Sam. Sam and the boys smile.

Glenn shakes his head at Travis and Freddy and says: "I'm impressed. You guys did good."

"Thanks," Travis and Freddy say with a smile.

"Let's walk and talk," Carl says to Sam, Travis, and Freddy. As he takes a step, Carl buckles. Sam catches him. Props him up as they head out. Feels good to be propped up, thinks Carl.

They walk. Carl limps.

"So you're a fed?" asks Travis.

"Yup," says Carl.

"That is so cool," says Freddy.

"Is Sam's old man really gonna get out of the house-goo?" asks Travis.

"Hoosegow." Sam laughs.

"Yup," says Carl sweetly.

"How cool is that?" asks Travis.

"Mad cool," says Freddy.

"I don't know what to say. I owe you guys big-time." Sam mists over, filled with much love for all three of them.

"Don't mention it," Travis and Freddy say together.

"You can mention it all you want as far as I'm concerned," wheezes Carl.

Sam chuckles as she shoehorns Carl into the front seat of her cab. Travis and Freddy climb in the back.

They ride. They talk.

"You understand," Carl says, "what you boys did was wrong, it was stupid, and it was dangerous."

"Sorry," Travis and Freddy say as meekly as they can.

"I should toss you both into a deep dark hole and throw away the key. You know that, don't you?" asks Carl.

"Yeah," Travis and Freddy say even meeker.

"I don't understand. Why did you do all this?" asks Carl.

Travis and Freddy look at each other.

"You tell him," says Travis.

"No, you tell him," says Freddy.

"No you," says Travis.

"No you," says Freddy.

"They came here," says Sam, "'cuz Trav's old man lost the farm."

"Well, actually the house," says Freddy, "but it's an expression, you know, *lost the farm.*"

"Yes, I'm aware of the expression," says Carl as Sam tries not to laugh.

"So they came here to win money to save his dad . . . and get to CyberWorld for their birthday—" says Sam.

"We're gonna be THIRTEEN," say Travis and Freddy.

"So I heard," says Carl.

"They have the same birthday," says Sam.

"Is that right?" says Carl.

"Oh yeah," say Travis and Freddy.

"Same day, same hospital, right across the hall from each other," says Sam.

"So you did all this 'cuz your family's in trouble?" asks Carl.

"Yeah," says Travis.

"And then we met Sam," says Freddy, "and we decided to help get her old man out of the goosehow—"

"Hoosegow," says Sam.

"Right," says Freddy.

"And then when we saw Johnny Large was gonna . . . you know, well, kill you," says Travis.

"We hadda do something," Freddy continues, "and that's when we, you know . . ."

"Saved your life," Travis and Freddy finish together.
Sam chuckles.

Carl feels a chuckle of his own, immediately blocks it, then says:

"What you boys did was illegal, and you could have been killed. You understand that?"

"Yeah," the boys say super-sheepish.

"You're never ever gonna break the law again, are you?" Carl asks like he really means it.

"No," say the boys.

"If you ever have a problem, you call me, anytime, day or night. Got it?" asks Carl.

"Yeah," say the boys.

"And no more gambling," he says to Travis.

"Yeah," says Travis.

"Promise," Carl makes them say.

"Promise," Travis and Freddy say as one.

They sneak a peek into the rearview mirror, where Sam flashes them a you-did-it look.

When Carl sees this, he falls a little more in love with Sam.

Travis nudges Freddy to ask Carl something. Freddy nudges Travis to ask Carl something. Furious nudging and nodding continue in the backseat.

Finally, Sam steps in and saves them.

"Hey, Carl, I think I speak for all of us when I say that we were wondering, uh, what you planned to do with the . . . uh, bag."

Travis and Freddy nod from the backseat.

"Ah yes"—Carl sighs—"the bag."

"I have an idea," says Sam.

"Yeah, I'm sure you do," says Carl.

"No," says Sam, "I don't want any of it, all I wanted was to get my dad out, and now he's gonna get out, so fair's fair, but . . . I thought maybe we could use the money to bail Travis's old man out, and if there's anything left, maybe start a little college fund for the Glimmer Twins, and possibly, I don't know, CyberWorld for their birthday."

The boys stare at Carl, trying to look as deserving as possible.

"I think that's a great idea," says Carl.

Their faces light up like Roman candles.

"But I can't," says Carl.

They deflate.

"This money's not yours. If I gave you this money, I'll be saying it's okay to take something that's not yours. And it's not. It's not okay. It's wrong. You two are smart; you can find other ways to make money. But not like this. You understand?" Carl asks.

"Yeah," Travis and Freddy say sadly.

Sam sees he's right. But she's sad, too.

"Once we get to the hospital," says Carl, "I'm sending you boys home, and I'll have all your stuff taken care of. But I'm gonna be checkin' up on you guys, and if I hear so much as a hint of funny business, I'm gonna personally kick your skinny butts from here to Walla Walla, Washington, and back. *Comprende?*"

"Yeah," Travis and Freddy say with a glum grin.

Sam parks the car, and they all get out except Carl, who tries, but fails miserably, a bolt of pure hurt slapping him back down with a face full of pain.

Sam, Travis, and Freddy manage to ease Carl out of

the tin-can cab. They stand in front of the hospital, these two best friends and these two lovers in love.

"Any questions?" asks Carl.

Travis and Freddy look at each other.

"Yeah," they say together.

"What is it?" asks Carl.

"Who is this guy Elvis?" the boys ask.

Sam cracks up laughing. Carl does the same, then grabs his side as the laugh vanishes. He reaches his unbroken arm out to the boys.

Travis shakes it.

Repeat with Freddy.

"You guys crack me up," Sam says through her laugh.

"Thanks, guys," says Carl. He leans in close and says in a hushed FBI voice: "Maybe in a few years there'll be a spot for you on the team."

"Really?" say Travis and Freddy a little too eagerly.

"But we never had this conversation." Carl winks.

"What conversation?" say Travis and Freddy.

Carl smiles small so it doesn't hurt.

Sam now moves into Travis and Freddy. The boys don't know what to do. They've never been hugged by a female other than Mrs. Best.

They want to hug. They want to run. They end up stuck in neutral. Sam draws them into her arms, Travis on one side, Freddy on the other.

The boys look at each other behind Sam's back, mid-hug, and smile with a shrug, thinking: This is sooooooooooo cool!

When the hug's done, the boys do some aw-shucks-ing.

"Thanks." Travis and Freddy beam big twin grins.

"Thank *you*," says Sam.

Thirty-seven minutes later Carl's being checked into the hospital, and Sam is talking to her dad on Carl's phone. He is so stunned by her news that he believes he's dreaming. When she finally convinces him he's not, he drops the phone. Pictures himself sitting in his daughter's kitchen, drinking a cup of her crazy tea, listening to Sam tell the story of the crazy Glimmer Twins.

Carl looks over at Sam and smiles.

Sam smiles back, just like she has in his dreams.

All of a sudden Carl doesn't hurt so much anymore.

Hanging, Chilling & Two Dead Boys Walking

Back at 395 Maple Street, in rainy Walla Walla, Washington, Travis's dad sits across the kitchen table from his wife.

"I'm sorry, I'll never do it again, please . . . forgive me," he pleads with all his heart and soul.

"I can't keep living like this," says Mrs. Best.

"I know. I can't either," says Mr. Best. "I've been thinking a lot . . . and I want to talk to you and Travis together."

"I don't know where he is," says Mrs. Best. "I'm a little worried about them, actually. When I talked to Freddy's dad this morning, he said he hadn't seen them. But of course he did seem a little, uh . . . distracted."

Mrs. Best hears noises from Travis's room.

What she doesn't know is that Travis and Freddy have just reentered the room by zip-lining in the upstairs window, after climbing up the big tree in the backyard.

Mr. and Mrs. Best head upstairs, where Travis and Freddy appear to be hanging and chilling, looking like they've been there all day.

This seems odd, so Mrs. Best asks:

"Where have you boys been?"

"Hangin'," says Travis casually.

"Chillin'," says Freddy casually.

"Where were you last night?" asks Mrs. Best.

"At Freddy's," says Travis, with a where-else-would-we-be? 'tude.

"But Freddy's dad said he hadn't seen you," she says.

"Well, you know my dad," says Freddy. "He doesn't know what century he's in."

"True." Mr. and Mrs. Best try not to laugh.

Silence.

Mrs. Best nods at her husband.

"Trav, Freddy," Mr. Best starts, "I'm really sorry about everything that . . . happened. And there are gonna be some big changes around here. Big changes. For one thing, I know I . . . I have a problem, and I'm gonna do something about it. I am. And I'm gonna promise you here and now, next year for your birthday we are going to CyberWorld, come heck or high water. Okay?"

"Okay," Travis and Freddy agree, racked nervous for so many reasons.

The phone rings.

Mr. Best goes into the hallway and answers it.

"Hello?" says Mr. Best. "Yes, that's me. Who is—" he starts to ask, but instead stops and listens.

"Uh-huh," says Mr. Best.

"Uh-huh.

"Uh-huh.

"I see.

"Yes.

"Yes.

"Yes.

"I understand.

"I see.

"Yes.

"Yes.

"Yes.

"I promise. Yes, I promise on Travis and Freddy's lives. Who is this?

"Hello?

"Hello?"

A puzzled look lives on Mr. Best's face as he hangs up and says:

"What the . . ."

He walks back into Travis's room with his puzzled face and says:

"That was the strangest call. . . ."

"Who was it?" asks Mrs. Best.

Neither parent has noticed that the mortified eyes of their son and his best friend are almost popping out of their young heads.

"I don't know, he wouldn't say," says Mr. Best.

"Well, what *did* he say?" says Mrs. Best.

"He told me that if I go to Gamblers Anonymous regularly for the rest of my life, starting now," says Mr. Best, "all my debts are gonna be paid in full. And all the credit-card bills. All of them paid in full. So long as I never gamble again."

Travis and Freddy exchange the tiniest glance two people can exchange.

"Probably a crank call," says Mrs. Best.

"No, he knew my Social Security number, and my mother's maiden name, and who I owe money to, every credit card, all my gambling debts—" says Mr. Best.

The doorbell rings.

Mr. and Mrs. Best give each other what's-next? looks.

"Are you expecting anybody?" Mrs. Best asks her husband.

"No," he says, "are you?"

The parents head down the stairs to answer the door.

Travis and Freddy, at the top of the stairs, hope against hope that Lady Luck will smile on them just one more time. They hear talking, but it's too soft to make out. Door shuts.

"Boys, could you come down here?" Mr. Best shouts sternly up the stairs.

Travis and Freddy look at each other condemned-criminal style, then trudge down the stairs like two dead boys walking.

"Something very strange is going on here." Mr. Best

does not look happy, holding a large envelope in his hand. "And I would like an explanation."

Travis and Freddy gulp.

"I have four first-class plane tickets, reservations at the CyberWorld Luxury Inn, and VIP passes to Cyber-World, all expenses paid, for this weekend. And there's a note here. It says: 'This is a little present to two of the most amazing young men I know. Happy Birthday, Travis and Freddy. P.S. Make sure to order room service.' What can you tell me about this, boys? And why did that man say to tell you the debts were taken care of?" Mr. Best asks the boys with a suspicious glare as he hands the envelope to Travis and Freddy.

Inside is Sam's black wig, a *Greatest Hits of Elvis Presley* CD, and an FBI Most Wanted sheet, starring Johnny "Large" Macaroni, with Considered Armed and Danger-ous and Reward for Information Leading to Arrest: $100,000 plastered on it.

Travis and Freddy try not to smile.

No luck.

"What can you tell me about this, boys?" asks Mrs. Best.

Travis stares at Freddy, no idea where or how to start.

"The truth?" asks Travis.

"The whole truth," says Mrs. Best.

With a deep breath Freddy starts.

"Okay, after you left the house, we decided to go to Vegas—"

"Only Freddy got his bag swiped—" adds Travis.

"With my iBrain mega-laptop in it. Only this super-cool chick kicked the guy's butt—"

"Sam—she's a cabby, she took us to the Excalibur—"

"We almost got caught hacking into the hotel computer—"

"Through the elevator phone—"

"We checked into the Elvis Suite, which was—"

"T-rex cool—" they say together.

"So Sam, she was trying to get her old man out of the housegoo—" says Travis.

"Hoosegow—" says Freddy.

"Right—"

"Then we won two hundred and fifty Gs—"

"Minus the thousand-dollar chip Sam tipped the dealer—"

"It was mad cool—"

"And then we had—"

"ALL YOU CAN EAT!!!" they say together.

"And then Johnny Large—"

"Who's this really tiny guy actually—"

"He found out—"

"We bamboozled the five grand from him—"

"And we got dangled—"

"Off the balcony of the thirty-fifth floor—"

"In our underpants—" they say together.

"By Moose—"

"And No Neck—"

"But then Carl—"

"He was the room-service guy—"

"Only he was actually undercover with the feds—"

"Very cool guy—"

"Way cool—"

"He saved our bacon—"

"And then Johnny Large tied him and Sam up—"

"They were gonna buy the bucket—"

"Eat with the fishes—"

"But we crawled through the ducts—"

"Only then the elevator came—"

"It was crazy gnarly—"

"Stupid gnarly!"

"I yanked him up outta the shaft—"

"He saved my life, seriously—"

"And then there were stink bombs—"

"And the cherry bombs—"

"And the maraschino cherries—"

"With the slingshots—"

"And we totally saved the day—"

"And they took Johnny Large away—"

"And Sam and Carl got together—"

"And Sam cleared her old man—"

"But Carl didn't let us keep the money—"

"Which way sucked—"

"Then they flew us home—"

"And that was it," they finish together with a flourish.

Mr. and Mrs. Best dead-stare at the two boys.

Then they burst out laughing.

"So, basically you sat home playing video games," Mrs. Best says.

Travis and Freddy grin at each other and say:

"Yeah, basically."

"Well, boys," says Mr. Best, "my dad always used to say, 'Never kick a gift horse in the mouth,' and I was never sure exactly what he meant by that, but it seems somehow appropriate here. I don't know what the heck happened here, but it looks like we better get our bags packed."

Travis and Freddy look at each other and shout: "WE'RE GOING TO CYYYYYYYYYYYBERRRRRRRRRRRRR-RRRRRRRRRRRRWOOOOOOOOOOOOOOOOOOOOOOO OOOOOOOOOOORLD!"